christopher osc

christopher oscar peña: Three Plays

how to make an American Son
the strangers
a cautionary tail

christopher oscar peña

LONDON • NEW YORK • OXFORD • NEW DELHI • SYDNEY

METHUEN DRAMA
Bloomsbury Publishing Plc
50 Bedford Square, London, WC1B 3DP, UK
1385 Broadway, New York, NY 10018, USA
29 Earlsfort Terrace, Dublin 2, Ireland

BLOOMSBURY, METHUEN DRAMA and the Methuen Drama logo are trademarks of
Bloomsbury Publishing Plc

First published in Great Britain 2024

A catalogue record for this book is available from the British Library.

A catalog record for this book is available from the Library of Congress.

ISBN: HB: 978-1-3504-2710-5
       PB: 978-1-3504-2709-9
       ePDF: 978-1-3504-2712-9
       eBook: 978-1-3504-2711-2

Series: Methuen Drama Play Collections

Typeset by RefineCatch Limited, Bungay, Suffolk
Printed and bound in Great Britain

To find out more about our authors and books visit www.bloomsbury.com
and sign up for our newsletters.

Contents

Foreword

Hugh Dancy

I first met chris peña in 2016, when I was lucky enough that he chose to write for me and a few others to perform as part of *The 24 Hour Plays* in New York. Obviously, therefore, the first thing you should know about chris is that he has great taste. It so happened that the event took place a few days after the election of that year, which loomed large over the mood and the output; all the writers addressed it, although for at least one it felt like an awkward shoe-horning of that mess into a much tidier, pre-conceived piece. Not chris. What he produced, in the few hours that the rules of the occasion allowed him, was a melange of open-hearted feeling, raucousness, magical realism, and sharp-edged satire, which was (I confess) initially bewildering to me; it was only mid-performance that I understood the artistry that had gone into creating the brew.

What I subsequently came to recognize, as I spent time with chris, is that the same qualities exist in him—he lives open-heartedly, perhaps one of the most social people I know (not in this case a euphemism for liking a party, although, sure), but he is also always processing. He's always listening! He's taking notes—not literally—and has found a place where transparency and slyness coexist. In other words, he's an artist. And, yes, it's no great surprise to recognize a writer in their plays or vice versa, but when said writer is asking—how am I allowed to fit in? Or not? How am I seen—or not? And in both cases, how much do I want that—then perhaps it also shouldn't be surprising that there's a shimmer to the work, and that just when you think you have it pinned down, it will move and shift into something different, more complex.

Hopefully this shift will, for you, not occur when you're on stage halfway through speaking the lines, because while enjoyable it's maybe a tad too humbling. Actually I take that back! I hope that is how you experience these plays! But regardless, onstage or off, heard, read, or performed, I know they are an experience you will carry with you.

a note on language

my parents are central american immigrans from honduras. english is their second language and they have strong accents. no way of hiding who they are (not that they should). when i was a kid i was up in ESL classes. for those of you who dont know, that stands for english as a second language. there is no shame in that. in fact, when white americans attack immigrants and act like theyre smarter, i always think, you know one language. barely. we know more than one, but you think youre better than us? thats confusing. i vividly remember as a kid having strong english literature skills. i was a lonely nerd so i was reading john grisham, christopher pike, stephen king, young star wars books, and yes, even danielle steel as early as 13. but when i went to school, i wasnt put in the "normal" english class, i was put in ESL. and i remember how my peers made me feel about that. i was made to feel like we were the stupid class. because of the way that we spoke. in high school, i was kicked out of AP english and put in the normal english class. when i was a very angry young person, i remember thinking im going to learn your own language and use it against you. because thats what language felt like. a weapon. except it was turned against us. immigrants. the other.

when we speak in our native tongues, we are often told that in america we speak english. the way we speak has no value here. at least thats what many try to make us feel.

people often ask me why i write the way i do. why i dont use grammer "correctly" and dont capitalize my name, or most things for that matter. the answer is, i wanted to dismantle the english language in my own small way. we are taught english in this perfectly grammatical way, but have you ever heard people speak that way? no. theyd sound like robots. so i wanted to write the way i hear the world. and thats often perfectly imperfect.

i write the way i do, to make space for others. even those that dont speak or sound "right." i wanted to make room for us, and validate our experiences, our voices. they are unique and singular and worthy.

i became a writer to make space for our narratives our lives and our stories. to make us exist. to remind us, that we are not alone, even if often, the world tries to make us feel like we are.

as we were putting together this collection, my editors reached out about what "corrections" i wanted to make to my original text. i thought long and hard about what i wanted to do. ultimately, i decided to leave it as it was, as i first heard it, mistakes and all. most things are in purpose. some are mistakes. in rehearsal, actors or other creatives in the room, have caught mistakes ive made. something spelled incorrectly. a character saying the wrong turn of phrase. at first, i would fix these things. then i began to realize, everyone i know, everyone in life, misspeaks all the time. so i decided that these should be character mistakes. things that make them who they are. so instead of "fixing" them, i wanted to honor the language of the individual.

the way i write language is meant to make room and welcome the musicality of the other. it shouldnt be a weapon. it should be celebrated.

a note on alienation

alienation: the state or experience of being isolated from a group or an activity to which one should belong or in which one should be involved

growing up immigrants were called resident aliens or non-resident aliens. reminding us we were other, or did not belong here, was built into the language of how we were spoken about. about how we were described. it was how we were named.

the theater is the first time i felt community, the first time i felt my family and didnt feel like an alien. i became a writer to honor the stories of all the people whod been told they were worthless, and invite them into the spotlight and center stage.

their voices, their language, our voices, our language, became center.

so this collection is dedicated to every actor who ever gave their time, their talent, their energy, their love to me, as i built these plays. thank you for lifting me up. the most important thing ive learned is that the business or fame wont be what validates me, it is your presence and your work in my life.

finally—

thanks to these directors for their contributions to my work

Leigh Silverman
Chay Yew
Jaime Castañeda
Kimberly Senior
Josh Hecht
John Sipes
Liesl Tommy
Liliana Blain-Cruz
Moises Kaufman
Ben Kamine
Evren Odcikin
Ben Villegas Randle
Gabriel Vega Weissman
May Adrales
Mark Armstrong
Patricia McGregor

Introduction

Mark Armstrong

For *The 24 Hour Plays*, where I am the artistic director, christopher oscar peña has written sixteen new plays since 2015. Over the course of two short plays, two short musicals, ten monologues, and two duologues, the word "love" (or a variation on it) appears 114 times.

The characters in his plays love deeply, wildly, unceasingly. They look for love in New York, in Idaho, on the faces of unseen others. They fall in love at least once a week, sometimes twice. They love when it rains and they love the look on your thoughtful face. They love this game we play and they love waking up with you.

These characters don't just love people, they love horchata lattes, "Walking in Memphis," and trains. They love three-day sleepovers, Bret Easton Ellis, the sunrise. They love kissing, smoking cigarettes in the morning thinking about heavy things. In one play, a poet covers all of New York City with love.

And they love you, always you.

As a theater director, I'm often asked how I choose plays to work on, what kind of material speaks to me. For years, I've answered: "I like plays that make me feel like I know the person who wrote it." Although we've never spoken about it, I know how important love is to chris. It's everywhere in his work.

With this love comes fear—the fear of not being loved back, not being loved enough. His characters are afraid they'll be left behind, that the things that make them happy will go away. They're afraid the person they love will abandon them, that they'll have that disease where they forget how to put together words. They're afraid of losing friendships, afraid this is the end. They're afraid they'll lose everything, afraid of telling you something true.

I'm afraid of these things because they've happened to me and I remember them. Through his work, I know they've happened to chris, too, and that he remembers them.

christopher oscar peña writes like a house on fire, like he's writing to outrun all his fears, like he's writing so much love into the world that maybe enough of it will wind up accruing to him. Although we've never spoken about this, either, I think he's winning. These plays are written from love, not fear. They've been created with and for his family of friends, a long list of comrades who've reflected his love back at him.

I'm proud to be among them and I hope all of you—readers and producers—will delight in these plays and help love run up the score.

Brooklyn, New York
August 2023

how to make an American Son

by christopher oscar peña

to

my father *for filling my head with dreams and telling me i could have all of them*

and

to

lee killam *for giving me the ocean*

how to make an American Son was originally commissioned by Yale Rep's (James Bundy, Artistic Director) Binger Center for New Theatre.

It had its world premiere at Arizona Theatre Company (Sean Daniels, Artistic Director) at the Temple of Music and Art in Tucson, Arizona running June 4 through June 25, 2022. It then moved to the Herberger Theatre Center in Phoenix, Arizona running June 30 to July 15, 2023.

It was directed by Kimberly Senior.

SCENIC DESIGN	Andrea Lauer
LIGHTING DESIGN	Reza Behjat
COSTUME DESIGN	Rodrigo Muñoz
SOUND DESIGN	Cricket S. Myers
FIGHT DIRECTOR/INTIMACY COORDINATOR	Alex J. Gould
DIALECT COACH	Micha Espinosa
PRODUCTION STAGE MANAGER	Glenn Bruner

The cast was as follows:

MERCEDES	Cristela Alonzo
RICHARD	Eddie Boroevich
RAFAEL	Alexander Flores
ORLANDO	Francisco Javier Gonzales
MANDO	Gabriel Marin
SEAN	Patrick Weber

how to make an American Son had its West Coast premiere as part of the American Generation Season at Profile Theatre (Josh Hecht, Artistic Director) in Portland, Oregon. Opening night was Saturday, June 10, 2023.

It was directed by Ben Villegas Randle.

SCENIC DESIGN	Megan Wilkerson
LIGHTING DESIGN	Blanca Forzan
COSTUME DESIGN	Sydney Dufka Forchielli
SOUND DESIGN	German Martinez
PRODUCTION STAGE MANAGER	Megan Thorpe
LINE PRODUCER	Jamie Rea

The cast was as follows:

MERCEDES	Crystal Ann Muñoz
RICHARD	Isaac Lamb
RAFAEL	Jonathan Hernandez
ORLANDO	Matthew Sepeda
MANDO	Jimmy Garcia
SEAN	Skyler Verity

characters

mando—honduran immigrant in his late forties/early fifties—"the father"

orlando—american-born honduran who reeks of privilege—"the son"

mercedes—american-born mexican woman in her thirties—"the help"

rafael—a newly arrived mexican immigrant—"the refugee"

sean—american-born white boy who thinks hes hot shit—"the dream"

richard—straight white guy in his early forties—"the enemy"

setting

spring 2001

        the silicon valley

bills.

an office
            heavy wooden desk
      a file cabinet
            its all very rustic—
                  very "of the earth"

on the walls
      we see

            tasteful knick knacks
            all from or representing
            HONDURAS
      maybe a wall clock in the shape of the country
            maybe a framed flag
                  perhaps a framed soccer—
                        i mean "futbol" jersey
      its all very patriotic—
            or maybe, its more
            nostalgic

                  on other parts of the walls
                        there are many
                        framed certificates
      "award in excellence"—multiple years
                  "highest quality"
                  "distinguished service"
                        all of these are made out to
            "ARMANDO CASABLANCAS"
                  and/or his company "DASH MAINTENANCE"

it is important to note
      that none of these are education based
or from educational institutes
            everything is in the details

right now
            mando casablancas
      white-looking (fair-skinned) immigrant latino with an accent
                  dressed in a suit and tie
            is scolding his son

orlando casablancas
a fifteen-going-on-sixteen teenager
hoodie and jeans
looks and sounds white gay
(looks and sounds gay?)

they sit on either sides of the desk
there is a piece of paper between them which **mando** *highlights*

mando
okay
and what about this one
on july 15th
for
wow
one hundred and eighty-four

orlando
wheres it from

mando
lets see
barnes and noble

orlando
theyre books

mando
you still buy books

orlando
theyre for school

mando
all of them

orlando
what do you have against reading i
could be out buying drugs instead
im buying books
i swear youre the only parent who complains that his kid is buying books

mando
youve never heard of a library
other parents send their kids to libraries

orlando
i want my own
in case i have to revisit
or
or
i like to highlight my favorite parts
and
you know
write notes
for later

im a very engaged reader dad
you should try it sometime

mando
numbers are all i care about

orlando
do you even have a favorite book

mando
yea
my checkbook

orlando
youre so funny
you should try stand-up
anyway i like books

> **mando** *looks at his son*
> *sighs*
> *then highlights the line*

mando
wheres the receipt

orlando
home
probably

mando
are you sure

orlando
yes

mando
i told you i need you to save all your receipts

orlando
i know i know

mando
make sure to give it to me later

orlando
can i go now

mando
were almost finished
okay what about this one from—

COACH
orlando
coach
again
three hundred and wow
orlando

orlando
what
i needed a new bag

mando
how many bags do you need

orlando
its for the new school year

mando
orlando

orlando
being gay is expensive

mando
so dont be gay

orlando
trust me
i tried

mando
is that true

orlando
what
no
ewww
no
of course not

mando
why am i the one who has to pay for your choices

orlando
weve been through this
its not a choice
and anyway
its a good bag

we have good taste

mando
this isnt funny

orlando
it costs to look this good

mando
then get a job like every other homosexual with nice clothes

orlando
you said if i kept my grades up i didnt have to work

mando
youre taking advantage

orlando
mom said i could

sigh

mando
thats coming out of your birthday present

orlando
BUT—

mando *shoots his son a look*

orlando
fine

mando
is that the bag

orlando *picks up the bag and shows it to his dad*

mando
its nice
not as gay as the last one

orlando
right dad
because having a bag is so straight

mando
im just sayin
its not like the last one
so flashy
people with money
they dont show it off all the time

this one
its good leather
should last you a long time
A LONG TIME
do you hear me

orlando
thanks dad

                              mando *highlights the line*

orlando
so i guess this probably isnt a good time to bring up the car

mando
what car

orlando
DAD
for my birthday
you said i could have a car

mando
i said maybe

orlando
DAD

mando
you can have your moms car

orlando
augh—
thats an old lady car

mando
its more than i had at your age

orlando
isnt that the point
for the next generation to be better

mando
THIS is better

orlando
whatever
SO

mando
so what

orlando
are we going to talk about the car

mando
not now

orlando
but you got my hopes up

mando
its good to have hopes
keeps you going

orlando
you said you were a man of your word

mando
i am
and i told you
it depends on how i do this year

orlando
but its almost my birthday

mando
maybe orlando
do you understand what maybe means
youre so smart
you dont know what maybe means
pull it up on the yahoo

orlando
but—

mando
fine
if we talk about it now
its going to be no
i suggest you stop while youre ahead
so do you want to talk about it now

orlando
you only turn sixteen once

a moment while **mando** *files the statement away*

mando
have you thought about where you want to go to college

orlando
i havent even applied yet

mando
dont save tomorrow to do
what you can do today

orlando
i have time

mando
you know if you stay close to home
that would be an incense to buy you a car

orlando
thats not fair
thats a bribe
youre trying to bribe me with a car
over college
and its IN-CEN-TIVE
work on your english
        mando *pulls out his wallet and starts throwing big bills at his son*
                                its a charming moment

mando
my friend abraham lincoln thinks my english is fine
my friends washington and hamilton do too
and oh look
heres benjamin
he thinks my english is perfect
oh here he is again
look at all the support hes showing

                                      all the benjamins keep flowing

orlando
i get it dad

mando
yea dont you forget it

orlando
oh i wont
when we go through next months credit card bill ill remember
you have plenty of benjamins to pay the bills

mando
me
yes
me
i earned them
not you

orlando
youre the one who always says
were family
whats yours is mine and whats mine is yours

mando
yes but im tired of this relationship
its all one way
what are you giving me

orlando
im an investment

mando
then i better cut my losses

theres a knock at the door

mando
come in

mercedes
american-born latina enters
she is **mandos** *right-hand woman*

mercedes
hey
i just got off the phone with jeff at genapro

mando
and

mercedes
and theyre committing to a three-year contract renewal

mando
three
even i havent gotten that
well done

orlando
mercedes

i am liking this new look on you
promoted to general manager
and already making boss moves

mercedes
thank you

                    a breath

mando
you did good
i knew you would

mercedes
and heres the copies you asked for orlando

orlando
thanks mercedes

mercedes
long book

orlando
i know right
i would have just ordered my own copy
but its out of print so—

mercedes
of course
also
heres the mastercard bill

orlando
i should call mom
see if shes done shopping
she can pick me up

mando
its okay
im leaving the office early today
i told her wed meet her at the mall for dinner

mercedes
hows school orlando

orlando
you know
the same
homework homework homework

we should get going so i can do that

mando
you can work while i finish up
just have to go over this bill

orlando
what time did you tell mom we were meeting her
dont want to make her wait

mando
fifteen minutes

orlando
so we should go

mando
its a five-minute drive

orlando
what about parking

mando
relax orlando
it will be fine

mercedes
i cant believe youre turning sixteen
i remember when you were in kindergarten
and look at you now

orlando
time flies

mercedes
ive been buttering your father up
i told him
at your age
you deserve a car

                              mando *pulls up a bill he is going over*

mando
what is this

mercedes
what

mando
this charge

orlando
can we finish this later

mando
do you have my credit card

orlando
what

mando
my mastercard

orlando
of course not
i have the visa

mando
because the mastercard is just for emergencies

orlando
right

> **mando** *pulls out his wallet*
> *he takes out several cards*

mando
i have my mastercard

mercedes
what is it

mando
there is a one thousand one hundred
there is an eleven hundred dollar charge on my card
do you know what thats about

mercedes
no

mando
its from—

> **mando** *drops the piece of paper on his desk*
> *he takes a deep breath and leans back in his chair*
> *he looks at* **orlando**

mando
mercedes can you step out a moment

orlando
oh no she can stay

mando
you want her to stay for the beating

mercedes
ill see you later

orlando
yea
it was good seeing you M

mercedes
mando dont forget—

mando
i know

she leaves the office

mando
you have something you want to tell me

orlando
i plead the fifth

mando
im being serious

orlando
i should probably get all the facts before i say anything

mando
eleven hundred dollars
from
ticketmaster

orlando
surprise

mando
how do you even spend that much money

orlando
it was supposed to be a surprise but
Madonnas playing san jose
i bought us tickets

mando
for who

orlando
you and mom
and me

mando
you took my card without asking
what
did you sneak into my room while i was sleeping

orlando
not exactly

mando
then

orlando
i memorized the number
last time

                        mando *just nods his head yes*

orlando
but its for us
for the family

mando
for the family

orlando
fourth-row seats
madonna
the queen
you like her

mando
not that much
you know
when i was a kid—

orlando
i know dad

mando
no actually
i dont think you do
have i ever hit you

orlando
dad

mando
answer me

orlando
no

mando
not once

orlando
not ever

mando
your grandfather
i remember this
a long long time ago
i took a chocolate from the
the
trucha
you know what a trucha is

orlando
no

mando
its
basically what the
its like a bodega

orlando
yea i get it

mando
when i got home he saw the chocolate in my hand
and he was so angry
he took me to the back
and you have to remember
this is honduras
so we dont have money for a nice yard or anything
there are these rocks out there
these little
theyre like pebbles
and he makes me go out back and he takes a chair
and he makes me kneel on the rocks
and hold the chair over my head

orlando
thats like child abuse

mando
not where i come from
and he pulls out his belt
and every time
every time im about to lower the chair
that belt
right across my back

orlando
i mean do you want me to say thank you
for like
for like
not beating me
for like
for like not being
you know
some third world
backwards
uneducated
backwards latino
is that what you want

                    mando *just shakes his head*

mando
where im from
where i grew up
they killed people like you

orlando
people like me

mando
the gays

orlando
yea
well
congratulations
you should be so proud
of where you came from

mando
where im from

people like you
they didnt exist
a person would disappear
or you would come across a dead body
cut up
what is that word
how do you say
mutilated
on the street
mutilated
no one would say anything
not one word
just keep walking
i came here because
that life
i didnt want that for you
i couldnt imagine a child
my child
growing up the way i did
but i look around
i look at this
i look at who i am
i look at your mother
and what weve made
what weve accomplished
and i think
i wonder
did i do the right thing
was it so bad
look at what it made us

orlando
im sorry okay
i should have asked
i know that
i should have asked

mando
maybe you forgot
what it was like for us
when you were little
or maybe you just didnt realize because we always gave you what you
needed

food
clothes
toys
if you needed it
you had it
and if you didnt need it
but we could give it to you
you had it
but it wasnt easy orlando

orlando
yea
well
things are different now

mando
sometimes i look at you
and i dont recognize you
this person that you are
this person that i made
weve made things too easy for you
you know your mother
she works hard
every day
cooking
cleaning
all the years weve been here
all the success weve had
but its still hard for her
she goes to the store
people talk to her like shes the maid
her english isnt perfect so they think she doesnt matter
but she doesnt go back
no
she stays
she stays
she goes to mervyns or jc penney
and where does she shop
in the clearance department
she never buys something nice for herself unless its on clearance
and you
a thousand dollars
just like that

orlando
whats the point of all this money if youre going to make me feel this bad
every time i spend it

mando
let me see your phone

orlando
what

mando
your phone

> **orlando** *hands over his phone*
>   *of course*
>   *its the most expensive model of whatever it is*

mando
your wallet

orlando
dad im not giving you my wallet

mando
youll give me whatever i ask for

> **orlando** *hands over his wallet*
>   **mando** *opens the wallet and pulls out*
>   **orlandos** *credit card*

mando
keep the wallet
its the card i want
oh
but you have it memorized
so heres the deal
you want a car
as of right now
the answer is no

orlando
seriously

mando
but if you do what i say
maybe
so
no phone

no credit cards
no tv
no movies
nothing

orlando
thats like
thats like
are you serious
thats like so
militant of you

mando
im not leaving any scars

orlando
this isnt fair
i mean
youre being so extreme
the punishment doesnt fit the crime

mando
finally

orlando
theres more

mando
every weekend
for the next month
youre coming to work for me

orlando
are you fucking kidding me

mando
que dijiste

orlando
im sorry
im just
in shock
or whatever

mando
thats what i thought

orlando
but i have plans

theres a movie and a school dance
and theres a game

mando
thats too bad
youre going to work off this debt

orlando
ill get a job at jamba juice or the movie theater

mando
thats not the point

orlando
i dont want to work in your office

> **mando** *starts to laugh*

mando
youre not going to work in my office

orlando
what does that mean

mando
youre going to do what i did to work my way up here
youre going to do what every single one of my employees does day in
and day out
to pay their bills
to feed their families
to eat and have a place to sleep
you are going to clean toilets
you are going to scrub shit
and scrub windows
and wash floors
the mop and the vacuum
the windex and the broom
for the next few weeks
these will be your best friends
youre going to do what i never made you do before
you are going to get your hands dirty
you are going to get on your hands and knees and work
W
O
R
K

work
you are my new janitor
and you are not going to say one word about it
                    and he doesnt
                            he doesnt say one word about it

mando
good
you start saturday

                                            scene.

debt.

mando *and* mercedes *in his office*

mando
and signotech

mercedes
they looked at the counter-offer and they accepted

mando
great
was there a lot of pushback

mercedes
the other offers they got were comparable but they didnt know the
quality

mando
why risk dropping us for someone slightly cheaper when weve been
giving them the gold
standard in service for years

mercedes
you were right

mando
good service
responsibility
loyalty
people appreciate that
good work

mercedes
i got renewals from sigmaform
humeticks
and mediabox as well

mando
good

mercedes
and ryan from procell said he went over the numbers and just had to get
board approval
but that he expects no problem and should get the contract to us by end
of week
she looks through her paperwork

mando
this is great work mercedes
you should be happy
i knew you were ready for this promotion
a moment
hows lucas

mercedes
hes
he cant find another job
hes starting to get frustrated

mando
he'll be okay

mercedes
i know its just

mando
what

mercedes
ive never seen him this way
this
en serio
its hard

mando
husbands supposed to work
cant be easy on his ego

mercedes
i dont know what to say to him anymore when i come home
ive stopped asking

mando
if he wants a job here

mercedes
thank you for offering
but you know him

mando
too good to be a janitor
even the latinos think theyre too good now
how very american of him
hed rather starve

mercedes
im
its embarrassing

mando
you know how people are

mercedes
mando
you know my cousin

mando
the one who just moved here from mexico
hes staying with you

mercedes
right
well thats it
he doesnt have anywhere else
anyone else
lucas
its getting tense at home
with neither of them working

mando
i can imagine

mercedes
and theres nowhere to send my cousin
rafael
and he has no money
mando
i hadnt asked
i didnt want to put you in this position
rafael
he needs a job
and he would take it
he would take this one
hes desperate
hes been asking me to ask you
i wouldnt normally but

mando
he can start on saturday

mercedes
really

mando
im giving antonio a few days off so we are short

mercedes
really
thank you that would
that would
it would just do so much for him
for us right now

mando
hes responsible right
youll vouch for him
you know what kind of ship i run around here

mercedes
of course
you have my word
if he messes up

mando
if

mercedes
he wont
but if he does
ill take full responsibility

mando
then its done

mercedes
theres just
i feel like i should tell you
hes—
you know
hes—
his papers

a breath

mando
you know we dont do things that way

mercedes
i know
thats why i didnt want to ask

but hes desperate

mando *takes a moment to think*

mando
okay
dont
dont say anything else
you do the books right
you do the hiring
the less i know the better

mercedes
are you sure

mando
i dont know what youre talking about

mercedes
okay
thank you mando

mando
this business is all i have
it provides for me and my family
i built it
from the ground up
and youve known us
since my kid was this tall
if youre not family
who is

mercedes
thank you

mando
set up a meeting with your cousin
i want to brief him

mercedes
okay

mando
is that all

mercedes
theres just one more
here

i thought you should see this
its repropsych

mando
reprosych

mercedes
theyre playing hardball
they turned down our offer
they said
they said they have better options

mando
did they give us a counter

mercedes
yes
its in the file

> **mando** *looks at the file*
> *he starts to laugh*

mando
are they serious
this wouldnt
this would barely cover our costs
chemicals
material
this would barely be enough for labor
we wouldnt even break even

mercedes
i know

mando
do you know who theyre looking at

mercedes
my friend
emilia

mando
the secretary

mercedes
yes
she said they want to go with max maintenance
theyre faster

and cheaper

mando
because they do bad work
because they rush

mercedes
im nervous mando
emilia said they seemed sure

mando
they cant be serious
weve been cleaning their building for over fifteen years
since before orlando was born
i remember
we got that account the same week mari told me she was pregnant
i was so happy

mercedes
what should i do

mando
call them up
there has to be a compromise we can reach

mercedes
ill do it right away

mando
dont look so worried
we have too many years of good work
of good history

mercedes
ill get that on the books now
                              she turns to go

mando
and mercedes
one more thing

mercedes
yes

mando
send antonio a bottle of whiskey
chivas
the big one

mercedes
you said you were giving him time off

mando
blanca is in labor
hes going to need that whiskey

                                                                    later

boys.

> *the parking lot of an affluent high*
> *school brand new toyotas*
> *hondas*

> *and more than a handful of*
> *bmws the occasional hand-me-down*
> *the students have nicer cars than the teachers*

orlando *is "casually" leaning against a chain-link fence*
he is "reading" a magazine

> *he looks around*
> *he checks his cell phone*
> *he looks around*

> *he looks at the magazine*

> *and then he sees something*
> *or someone*

> *and poorly tries to look like hes reading*

> *a hot white guy*
> *approaches in a white tee and gym shorts*
> *hes probably on the soccer team or plays football*
hes clearly a hot, entitled fuck
> *reeks of privilege*
> *and* **orlando** *loves him*
> *the white guys name is* **sean**
> **sean** *is goals as fuck for* **orlando**

sean
hey cutie

> **orlandos** *heart just jumped*
> **sean** *is basically mocking*
> *him but* **orlando** *doesnt care*
> *like press—any attention is good attention*

orlando
oh hey

sean
what are you still doing here

orlando
waiting for my ride

sean
waiting for mom

orlando
shut up sean
im waiting for my friend
shes on the dance committee
theyre having a meeting

sean
cool cool
what are you reading

orlando
just this article on this band i love

sean
some boy band

orlando
you probably dont know them

sean
ive heard of the backstreet boys

orlando
youre so stupid
theyre called
rage against the machines

sean
shut the fuck up

orlando
what
you know them

sean
know them
theyre my fucking favorite   *none of this is new information to*
                                            orlando

orlando
i like that stuff
rage
foo fighters

sublime

sean
i didnt know that about you

> *trust me*
>> *no one does*

orlando
well
im full of surprises

sean
whats your favorite song

> **orlando** *doesnt have an answer*
>> *cuz he aint know shit*

orlando
all of them
real fans dont have a favorite

sean
i like killing in the name

orlando
yea
thats kind of obvious

sean
fuck you

orlando
just saying

sean
you know theyre playing here this weekend

orlando
obviously

sean
i tried to get tickets but that shit sold out so quick
i looked on ebay but the cheapest tickets were like four hundred bucks
its bullshit

orlando
oh
i got some

sean
you do

orlando
theyre my favorite band

sean
im fucking jealous

orlando
hows your girlfriend

sean
tiffany

orlando
yea

sean
shes not my girlfriend

orlando
oh
i see you guys together a lot

sean
yea she gives good head

orlando
oh wow

sean
you blushing

orlando
shut up no im not

sean
yeah you are
i make you blush

orlando
please

sean
you like giving head

orlando
whatnoshutup

sean
or are you a virgin

orlando
i didnt say that

sean
oh so youre a little slut then
perfected the craft of fellatio
you good at giving head

orlando
sean

sean
i bet you are

orlando
youll never know

sean
oh what
you too good for me
youd turn me down

orlando
i didnt say that either

>   **sean** *gets really close to* **orlando**
>   *its weird but also a little sexy*

sean
then what

orlando
arent you straight

>   **sean** *gets so close to* **orlando**
>   *theres only fabric between them*

sean
mostly

>   **sean** *starts to laugh and pulls away from* **orlando**

sean
i gotta go

orlando
hey sean

sean
what

orlando
wanna be my date to the concert

sean
i thought youd never ask

> **sean** *starts to walk away*
> *just when we think hes gone*
> *he turns for one last look*

sean
you coming

> **orlando**
> *surprised as fuck*
> *grabs his shit and runs after* **sean**
> *its on bitches*

later

foreign.

> *we are in the very sterile, corporate office*
> *of repropsych—a couple desks, nothing particularly*
> *appealing about this place*

> *we see three people*
> **orlando**, *in a janitorial uniform*
> **mando**, *in jeans and a polo, his "casual"*
> *weekend look and a young latino man*
> *also in a uniform dark skin*
> *sexy as fuck*
> *couldve been a soccer player*
> *his name is* **rafael**
> **mando** *is teaching the two guys how to "clean" the windows*

mando
and then you go back just before the line and
> *he demonstrates*
you see what im doing with my arm
this motion
makes it faster but precise
its important that you keep moving but dont sacrifice quality
if you mess up go back

orlando
we get it

mando
show me

orlando
are you serious

mando
youre at work right now

orlando
forced labor

mando
orlando im not playing
> **rafael** *silently watches*
> *not sure what to do*

orlando
look
see
i can do it

mando
that spot right there

orlando
its fine

mando
its not

orlando
youre being a dictator

mando
look
take this seriously and do this right
orlando
no estoy jugando
entiendes

orlando
okay

mando
okay

orlando
i said okay

                    mando *turns his attention to* **rafael**

mando
entendistes todo

rafael
si

mando
tienes preguntas

rafael
no

mando
vaya pues
i will stop by in an hour

if you mess up
im making you start over

orlando
we get it
> **mando** *hands a squeegee to* **rafael** *and a duster to* **orlando**

mando
make sure to get under the table orlando

orlando
bye

> *he goes*
> *silence for a moment as the two men work*
> > **rafael**, *of course, is taking his job very seriously*
> **orlando** *is basically not*

orlando
so you just moved here

> *nothing*

i said did you just move here

> *nothing*

oh duh
im so stupid
you probably dont know any english

> > **orlando** *works a bit*
> *gets bored*

cuando llegaste

> *oh hey!*
> > **orlando** *speaks spanish*
> *and surprisingly ITS GOOD*

eres primo de mercedes
no me escuchas
> *finally* **rafael** *turns around*

rafael
estamos trabajando

orlando
okay then
wow

they work in silence some more
the following is more to himself than anyone specifically

orlando
immigrants
i mean
i would just think
i dont know
maybe like be friends with the boss's son
like duh
like dont make enemies with the person with the most power in the
room
common sense
this is why so few of you actually get ahead
its the american way
i just like
i dont understand you know
like why come here and then like
not play by the rules of america
it feels
i dont know
like counterproductive or something
like if youre going to come here
like figure it out you know
otherwise stay there
stay there
duh
i just
it blows my mind
immigrants come here and then like dont want to adapt
when im like
im like
isnt the reason you came here because you didnt like it where you were
from
so like
why try to retain that
that
that
way of life
no
yes
structure

culture
i dont know
like im just saying
you come here
for what
for what
to get ahead
to succeed
to have a better life
like im not anti-immigrant
im not
duh
like i get it
america is pretty awesome or whatever
but then like
learn the american way
be friends with the boss's son
learn english
you know what i mean
learn english
its like the bare minimum—

> **rafael** *cuts* **orlando** *off*

rafael
i know english

orlando
oh

> *a breath*

i didnt know

rafael
yes theres a lot you dont

orlando
how did you learn—

rafael
i know americans think were all stupid
but they teach us at school now
and we watch american television

orlando
you werent responding

rafael
i came here to work
not to make friends

orlando
oh
i just thought talking would make the work go faster

rafael
working would make the work go faster

orlando
yep i guess youre right

they work in silence

orlando
when did you come here

rafael
last month

orlando
oh
so recent
welcome

rafael
thanks

orlando
where do you live

rafael
con mercedes

orlando
youre related

rafael
yes

orlando
cool
have you been to the city yet

rafael
the city

orlando
san francisco
the metreon is my favorite

rafael
i dont know what that is

orlando
maybe we can go sometime
when we get out of this hellhole

rafael
thats nice but probably not

orlando
ouch

rafael
sorry
im just honest

orlando
i was just trying to be nice
you dont have to be—

rafael
they told me not to get close to you

orlando
what
why
who

rafael
i dont want to waste time
they said i should be careful around you
to stay away from you

orlando
to stay away from me

rafael
to be careful around you
youre the boss's son

orlando
what does that matter

rafael
didnt you just say it did

orlando
i mean it does but i dont understand how it could hurt—

rafael
im not supposed to tell you anything personal
any secrets
this is work—

orlando
you have secrets—

rafael
i mean—
thats not what i
never mind
im hear to work okay
WORK

                              orlando *seems sad and confused*

rafael
im sorry
i just
i shouldnt have told you that

orlando
fuck that
who said that
why
i dont understand
who said that
my dad

rafael
no

orlando
it was my dad wasnt it
fuck him

rafael
wow

orlando
what

rafael
you talk about your dad that way

orlando
whatever

rafael
in mexico
lets just say that would never happen

orlando
I KNOW

a moment

orlando
i cant believe he would tell you that
trying to isolate me and shit

rafael
it wasnt him

orlando
then who was it
theres no one—
mercedes

                        rafael *doesnt say anything*

orlando
why would mercedes
is it because im gay

rafael
youre gay

orlando
you didnt know

rafael
no

orlando
oh
well yea
i am
is that weird to you
does that make your mexican sensibilities uncomfortable

rafael
you dont know what youre talking about

orlando
then enlighten me

rafael
you have no idea how lucky you are
the way you talk
they were right about you

orlando
what does that even mean

rafael
youre not like us

orlando
mercedes said that

                    a moment
                            hes never considered this fact

orlando
when i was in second grade
i had a pretty bad accent
there was this program
GATE
gifted and talented education
it was where all the smart kids go
my parents thought i should be in that program
i was smart
i was smarter than everyone i knew
but because of my accent
my bad english
they put me in esl
do you know that that is

rafael
no

orlando
english as a second language
its where they put the stupid kids
thats really what it meant
i came home one day and
and

mercedes
shes the one who helped me with my english
to make it better
now
youd never know
i cant believe she would say that

rafael
we just
i have to be careful around you

orlando
why would she say that
shes like my older sister
shes family

rafael
no shes not

orlando
ive known her my whole life

rafael
it doesnt matter
youre the boss's son

                    rafael *starts to go*

orlando
where are you going

rafael
some of us dont get paid to stand around
some of us have to work

                    and hes gone

                                        later

time.

> *later that evening*

> **orlandos** *bedroom—*
> *the posters on the wall dont exactly express "rage Against the*
>   *machine" but instead*
>   *john mayer*
>   *justin timberlake*
>   *no doubt*
>   *as you do*

> **orlando** *lies in bed on his laptop*
>   *he is searching for something*
>   *he finds something*
>   *he pulls out his cellphone and makes a call*

orlando
hey
hi
im actually calling about your post online
the rage tickets
im wonderfing if you still have them or
oh okay
thanks anyway

>   *he hangs up*
>   *scrolls through his laptop and finds another post*
>   *dials*

orlando
hi yes
im calling about the tickets you posted
yes
you still have them
okay great
on your post
you said you were selling them for three hundred
thats for the pair right
oh
oh
each
yea
wasnt face value seventy—

yea i know theyre
right
would you be willing to negotiate
i understand
hey man im just asking you dont gotta be a dick about it
whatever
dick

> *he hangs up*
>
> *just then there is a knock on his door*
> *he slams his laptop shut and throws it on the floor*
> *he hurriedly picks up a book next to him and starts to read*
> *if we could see the title you would see its james baldwins giovannis room*

orlando
yes

mando
can i come in

orlando
its your house

> **mando** *opens the door*

mando
its our house

orlando
ownership implies control
could i sell this house

mando
do you want to

orlando
thats not the point

> *a moment*

mando
can i join you

orlando
its your bed
you paid for it

mando
good point

> **mando** *approaches the bed*

mando
scoot over then

> **orlando** *scoots over some*
> **mando** *lies in bed next to him*
> *he crosses his arms*

mando
what are you reading

orlando
a book

mando
i can see that
which one

orlando
not one you know

mando
how do you know that

orlando
you never graduated high school
ive never seen you pick up a book a day in my life
im pretty sure its a safe bet to make

mando
youre right
but im doing okay arent i
have more money than most of your well read "intellectuals"

orlando
why do you say it like that

mando
books
all you do in school is keep your head in the clouds
everyone thinks theyre so educated but they cant balance a checkbook
have no practical skills to get a job
maybe i dont know who
> *he grabs the book*

Baldwin is
but the nice thing is
i can afford not to

orlando
you sound like a republican

mando
proud to be one

orlando
gross
gross
thats gross dad

mando
all democrats want is to spend my money
you like looking good right

orlando
what does that have to do with anything

mando
you say you have to look good
have the right clothes and the right car and the right shoes and the right
    bag
i dont know if you noticed
but looking good is expensive
you want me to be a democrat
okay
but then you have to get used to being poor

orlando
I WOULD NEVER
poverty does not suit me

mando
all these things you want
the bags and the shoes and the nice car
you dont need them orlando
youre just spoiled and irresponsible
                    orlando *goes back to his book*

mando
how was your day

orlando
fine

mando
thats it

orlando
im reading dad

i have to keep up with school
you know
im trying to be educated

mando
okay

                    they lay in silence for a bit

orlando
are you seriously just going to lay there

mando
whats wrong with that
im tired
i want to hang out with my son
whats the point of working so hard if i cant even do that

orlando
whatever

                    they lay in silence

mando
are you still mad at me

orlando
whatever dad

mando
okay

orlando
okay what

mando
im not going to bed until you stop being mad at me

orlando
sucks for you

                    orlando *puts his book down*
                    and turns his body to his side away from his dad
                        like hes going to sleep

orlando
good night

                    they lay there in silence
                        then **mando** *sneak attack tickles* **orlando**

orlando
WHAT IS WRONG WITH YOU
stop tickling me

mando
if i cant go to bed than you cant go to sleep

orlando
youre such a psycho

mando
we never go to bed angry
you know that

orlando
this is so unfair
you cant control the way i feel
youre a dictator
a tyrant

mando
a dictator
i like that
i am the king of the castle

orlando
youre not funny

mando
i think im funny

they lie there

mando
you did good today
a little slow start
but you got better
mercedes checked your work and she said you did good

orlando
cool

mando
if you keep it up
ill cut your time short

orlando
okay wait
can we compromise

mando
there are no compromises in punishments

orlando
please
can we barter

mando
barter
what is that word

orlando
negociar

mando
oh negotiate

orlando
yes
a word you understand

mando
nope
you have no power
i have all the power
therefore i dont need anything

orlando
come on dad
please
this is a business tactic
see
im learning
lets negotiate

mando
what is your proposal

orlando
there is a concert this Saturday

mando
vos y tus conciertos
no mas

orlando
come on dad
i already bought the tickets

mando
what

orlando
im sorry okay
i charged them on the card before you grounded me

mando
you are unbelievable
we are selling the tickets

orlando
dad please
let me go this saturday and you can extend my punishment on the back
    end
like a loan
a loan on time

mando
i dont like loans
thats not the way we do things in this family
no loans
no debt
i dont want you to ever owe anybody anything

orlando
were family

mando
even in family
money has a way of ruining relationships

orlando
youre my dad
and im borrowing time

mando
youre so young
you dont realize yet
how valuable that is

orlando
please

mando
negociando con mi hijo para mas tiempo
que loca es la vida

orlando
please please please

mando
okay
on one condition

orlando
im listening

mando
if you do excellent work saturday
you can go

orlando
yes yes yes thankyouthankyouthankyou

mando
not good work
not great work
EXCELLENT WORK
no complaining

orlando
YES

mando
and your extra weekend of punishment
you have to spend it with me

orlando
augh dad

mando
deal or no deal

orlando
deal deal deal

                              orlando *hugs his father*

orlando
now we can go to sleep

mando
no we cant

orlando
why not

mando
because now im angry

                               orlando *laughs*

                  mando *sighs*

                       always getting played by his son

                                    later

work.

> orlando *and* **rafael** *at work*
> > **rafael** *is cleaning the windows*
> > **orlando** *is dusting*
> > *hes killing it*

rafael
you seem happy today

orlando
i am

rafael
its almost like youre enjoying yourself

orlando
making the best out of a bad situation
i mean not bad—
just—

rafael
i know what you mean
> **orlando** *smiles at him apologetically*

orlando
do you miss it

rafael
what

orlando
home

rafael
this is my home now
better not to think about it

orlando
sorry i didnt mean—

rafael
its okay
> *they work in silence*

rafael
have you ever been to honduras

orlando
a long time ago

rafael
oh yes

orlando
when i was a kid
i think maybe when i was like five or six
and then maybe again when i was nine
something like that

rafael
did you like it

orlando
i remember some things
but not very much to be honest

rafael
its very beautiful

orlando
youve been

rafael
of course
we travel too you know
we leave our own countries

orlando
im sorry
thats not what i meant
sorry
will you tell me about it
                              a breath

rafael
did your dad ever take you to la ceiba
they have the most beautiful beaches
the water
clear
so so clear
ive still never seen something so beautiful
and these plants
i remember these plants
i forget what they were called

the leaves stretched out like this

he shows **orlando** *with his hand*

but then when you touched them

orlando
they would close like this

rafael
yes yes

orlando
i do remember those
running around touching them all
watching them close
like magic

rafael *smiles*

rafael
i miss those

orlando
thats so weird

rafael
what

orlando
how we share this memory
but dont

rafael
some things are just
its your culture you know
its in your roots

orlando
nerd

rafael
im—very sentimental

orlando
can i ask you a question

rafael
okay

orlando
i dont want to seem like some stupid american making assumptions

rafael
okay

orlando
why did you come here

rafael
same reason everyone else does
for a better life

orlando
stock answer

rafael
stock answer

orlando
it means generic
it means youre not being honest
it means the easy way out

                            rafael *looks torn*

rafael
my family wasnt so accepting of me

orlando
sorry

                          they continue to work

orlando
i have a date tonight
this guy i never thought would be into me
he—
maybe i underestimated myself
thats why im happy i guess

rafael
youre lucky
your father
hes not like mine

                        orlando *senses something*

orlando
i told my mom and
do you know what she said

rafael
what

orlando
its okay that you are gay
but if you are going to bring a guy home
at least make sure hes latino

rafael
thats nice

orlando
did you have a girlfriend back home

                              rafael *looks conflicted*

rafael
no
i—
no

orlando
oh
okay

rafael
what are you doing for your date

orlando
were going to this concert
rage against the machine
do you know them

rafael
rage against—

orlando
the machine

rafael
no
this band
i dont

orlando
theyre not really my thing either

rafael
then why are you going

orlando
the guy

rafael
oh

orlando
he loves them

rafael
i understand

orlando
what do you listen to

rafael
janet jackson
she is my favorite

orlando
i love janet

rafael
me too

orlando
whats your favorite song

rafael
you know this song
together again

orlando
yeah totally

rafael
i love the dancing

orlando
thats the way love goes is my favorite

rafael
yes
that song is so beautiful
                    maybe they sing a bit together

orlando
who else do you like

rafael
i love michael
of course
and prince
prince is great
whitney houston

orlando
oh whitney

rafael
and madonna
and celine dion
i LOVE celine dion

orlando
wow
your music taste is very
                    he stops himself

rafael
what

orlando
never mind

              a tense moment
                    they continue cleaning
orlando *watches* **rafael**
          maybe notices how beautiful he actually is for the first time
      notices his arms
          his tan skin

orlando
ive never dated a latino guy before

rafael
oh

orlando
its not because i dont want to
or im not attracted to them
thats what i told my mom
its just
theyre never attracted to me for some reason you know

rafael
oh

orlando
yea
i dont know
maybe if i had like an opportunity
but
yea
anyway
do you work out a lot

rafael
what

orlando
i just realized
your arms
youre like super-fit
you must work out a lot
maybe thats what im so bad at this job
im so weak

rafael
youre just not applying yourself
this job is the workout

orlando
maybe if i keep doing this ill have arms like you one day

rafael
maybe

                    rafael *is flattered*

rafael
your arms are fine

orlando
fine

rafael
i didnt mean

orlando
asshole

rafael
im sorry i didnt mean to offend you—

orlando
im just joking rafael
it was a joke
im not really mad

rafael
oh
okay
yes
a joke

orlando
were friends right

> **rafael** *doesnt know*

rafeal
friends

> *as* **rafael** *keeps working*
> **orlando** *watches him*   *developing*
>   *a crush*
> **orlando** *goes over to* **rafael**

orlando
here
you missed a—

> *they are intimately close together*
> *there is an electricity*
>   *an*
>   *obvious*
>   *SPARK*
>   *between them*
> *they can each feel the others breath*
>   *their hearts pounding*

orlando
spot

> **orlando** *wipes the spot*

rafael
thank you
we should keep moving if you want to finish early enough for your date

> *he goes*

> **later**

sweat.

orlando *and* **sean** *in* **seans** *car*

sean
that was fucking epic
that drum solo—

orlando
when his kit—

sean
fucking right

orlando
the crowd just went—

sean
NUTS

orlando
it was electric

sean
you caught me off guard

orlando
what

sean
you impressed me

orlando
what do you mean

sean
when i wanted to jump in that mosh pit
i was sure youd bitch out

orlando
what
no
why

sean
you just dont seem like the type

orlando
well im full of surprises

sean
yeah you are
you went in there like a fucking beast
surprised your glasses survived

orlando
i almost lost them for a second
this guy almost stepped on them
but i was fucking quick
just shoved him out of the way
fucking pushed him
my animal instincts
i guess they kicked in
it was like my blood
i dont know
it felt electric

sean
i love that feeling

orlando
youre so sweaty

sean
it makes me feel alive

orlando
yeah

sean
i probably stink though
sorry about that

orlando
nah you smell—

sean
what

orlando
just i dont know like a dude
like a man

sean
yea
you like it

orlando
what if i do

sean
im glad

> **orlando** *looks at* **sean**
> > **sean** *is daring him with his face*
> *but* **orlando** *breaks*

orlando
i loved watching him drum

sean
hes my idol

orlando
i like watching you drum

sean
oh yeah

orlando
your bands alright
matt—

sean
hes a shit singer

orlando
but when you drum
i dont know
its like
youre in your element
watching you take it all out on the drums
all that energy all that aggression

sean
you like that

orlando
i guess
you know how to handle your sticks
> **sean** *laughs*

orlando
i mean
thats not—

sean
i know what you meant

orlando
no thats not—

sean
youre right
i do

> **sean** *shoots* **orlando** *another loaded look*
> *he readjusts himself in his seat*
> *opening himself up*

orlando
this traffic fucking sucks

sean
yeah its always a fucking nightmare getting out of this parking lot
i dont even try anymore
i just wait till everyone leaves
but i come prepared

> *he leans over* **orlando** *reaching out for his glove compartment*
> *they are THIS close*

orlando
youre dripping

sean
what

orlando
your sweat

sean
oh sorry man

orlando
its okay

> **sean** *opens the glove compartment and pulls out a joint*

sean
its the best time to smoke
wait out the traffic
just sit here
in the outdoors
looking at the stars

sean *lights up*

orlando
but you have to drive

sean
its cool man
i drive better when i smoke

orlando
im—

sean
what

orlando
im just
i dont know
uncomfortable

sean
what happened to that guy who surprised me and lived on the edge
this is who i thought you were
boring

orlando
its just
my friend
he got in a car accident so—

sean
oh
im an asshole
sorry man

orlando
its—

sean
here ill stop

orlando
no
its okay

sean
you sure

orlando
yeah
its nice
just sitting here

sean
cool

> **sean** *smokes*
>> *he inhales*

sean
we can just sit here for a while
smoke
and then
sober up
until youre comfortable

orlando
thanks

sean
might be a while though

orlando
its okay
i dont have any other place to be

sean
i guess youll just have to find a way to entertain me

orlando
what

sean
keep me busy

> **sean** *looks at* **orlando**
>> *he looks down at his crotch*
> *he readjusts as he does*
>> *its pretty obvious*
> **orlando** *is too scared*
>> *hes not sure what to do*

sean
youre not aggressive enough

orlando
i dont—
what

sean
if you want something you have to take it

orlando
i dont—

                            sean *grabs* **orlandos** *hand and puts it on his crotch*

orlando
oh

sean
isnt this what you came for

                            orlando *reaches out and tries to kiss* **sean**

sean
i dont kiss

orlando
at all

sean
maybe if you earn it

                            sean *guides* **orlandos** *head down to his crotch*
                                  sean *takes another hit from the joint*

            inhales

                exhales

                    closes his eyes

       and leans

             his

                      head back

                             later

latinos.

> **mando** *working late at the office*
> *a knock at the door*

mando
come in

> **mercedes** *walks in*

mando
youre still here
i told you to go home a while ago

mercedes
i know
i was going to wait and give rafael a ride home

mando
hes been doing great work

mercedes
good im glad you think so

mando
i like him
he works hard
some of these guys
remember ronaldo
showed up to work hung over
then asking me for an advance on his paycheck
these guys
they dont learn
they come here
for what
to party
to drink
and then he asks me for money
tells me his daughter and wife
son of a bitch
out throwing money away drinking
and then im supposed to help him
people like that
they dont get ahead
never
they are always asking for more more more

im the president of this company and i stay and work late and these guys
out partying
i dont understand them
thats why everyone hates latinos in this country
think they are all on welfare
but rafaels been good
he has his head in the right place

mercedes
good good
im glad to hear it
and thank you for
you know
giving him the opportunity

mando
of course mercedes
i trust you

mercedes
is that the reprosych file
can i help with that

mando
no no
all your numbers are good
im just going over them again

mercedes
are you sure we shouldnt just take their counter

mando
absolutely not
wed be working for free
we wouldnt make any profit

mercedes
but wed keep the account

mando
but for how long
when the contracts up he'll twist our arm again and end up going
somewhere else
this new guy from repropsych
whats his name

mercedes
richard

mando
richard
he needs to respect the process
weve been cleaning that building for sixteen years now

mercedes
thats a long time

mando
it was one of the first accounts we landed

mercedes
when i spoke to him—
it—
he didnt really listen to a word i said
said he would only talk to you
he was just so

mando
what

mercedes
nothing

mando
que paso

mercedes
arrogant
im not—
never mind

mando
i know the type
you have to stroke their ego
pendejos

mercedes
yea exactly
he was a fucking asshole
every time i think—
things dont change

mando
maybe they do
maybe they dont

you just have to learn the rules of the game
and then do what you can to work around them

mercedes
im worried mando
this could be bad for us
if he doesnt take the deal—

mando
he will
trust me
have faith
trust the system
i know this kind of guy
he just wants me to meet him in person

he laughs coldly

mercedes
what

mando
he just wants to prove he can get me there
meet him in person
at his business
on his terms
and grovel
he just wants to exercise his power

mercedes
its disgusting

mando
it doesnt matter
it means nothing to me and everything to him
so ill go
ill shake his hand
ill thank him for his business
thats all that matters anyway

mercedes
mando there is—

mando
yes

mercedes
rafael told me that orlando wanted to show him around

mando
show him around
like hang out

mercedes
yes
but of course i told him no
to say no to orlando
that it would be inapprorpriate
but i wanted to tell you
in case orlando said anything
i told rafael he has to work and—

mando
its okay

mercedes
what

mando
did orlando really ask
really
it was his idea

mercedes
yes

mando
thats nice
thats good
esta bueno
maybe hes learning something
im glad
hes finally paying attention
opening up to
showing someone with less means
this is good

mercedes
are you sure

mando
why wouldnt i be
orlando is a good kid

he doesnt party or hang with the wrong kids
he'll be a good influence on rafael
keep him out of trouble
this is good
maybe my son is learning something after all
maybe he is the son of his father
is that how you say that
the apple doesnt fall far from the tree

mercedes
hes his fathers son

mando
well of course he is

mercedes
thats the saying

mando
it doesnt even make sense
americanos puta
always trying to make things more complicated

he goes back to his paperwork
mercedes *stands there unsure*

later

dads.

> *the next day*
> *outside*
> > *the front of a corporate office building*
> *the door opens*
> > **mando** *walks out with a white guy in his early forties*
> > > *the white guy is wearing khaki shorts and a polo*
> *well call him* **richard** *or, you know,* **dick**
> **mando** *holds the door for them as they walk out*
> > *they are mid-conversation*

(NOTE:
**in production, when you get to the underlined dialogue in this scene,
staging will help with the chaos that should ensue on stage
characters are half-listening
they want to be in more than one conversation
the gist of information necessary for this scene is here
but the actual choreography of how its revealed should be discovered
and choreographed in production)**

mando
i appreciate you taking the time, mister hinkle

dick
i told you
call me dick

mando
i never understood that

dick
what

mando
your first name is richard
shouldnt it be rich

dick
rich was my father

mando
so youre rich junior

dick
i am my own man

mando
but how do you get dick out of richard
there not even the same letters

dick
its just the way it is

mando
ive been here for thirty years
i know my english
but some things will never make sense to me

dick
i guess they wont

                    dick *inspects the glass door*

dick
can you just wipe this down on your way out
there are some fingerprints

mando
of course
someone must have touched the door recently

dick
must have

mando
like i said
even as my company has grown
we still think of it as a mom and pop shop
the personal connection
the personal work
its important to me
if i tell you we are going to do something
you can be certain we will
i personally make sure of it

dick
thats good to hear
your competitors
theyre very aggressive
their prices were better—

mando
but not the quality

dick
but i know how important this account is to you
and that means something to me
so
i want you to know i went to bat for you
my colleagues werent sure the quality of service was different enough
that it warranted the
price hike
but
dont disappoint me

mando
of course of course
i understand
thank you for sticking by us
this partnership is important to me
im very grateful to you

dick
have your assistant send over the contracts tomorrow
what was her name
maria

mando
mercedes

                                              dick *laughs*

mando
what

dick
no never mind

mando
oh come on my friend
you must tell me

dick
her name
champagne
diamond
these names—
but she is beautiful
smart man
having a secretary like that

mando
shes actually my general manager

dick
oh

mando
she has worked very hard for me to get there

dick
im sure she has
she come here with you

mando
what do you mean

dick
is she from—
where are you from

mando
honduras

dick
yes there

mando
shes actually mexican

dick
well
thats not surprising
i should have known

mando
but she was actually born and raised here

dick
really

mando
born in oakland
went to school in berkeley
hard worker
smart woman
she'll be hiring us one day

dick
well i dont know about all that

just then the door opens and **orlando** *pops out*
hes wearing a janitors uniform

mando
orlando

dick
this one of your guys

mando
this is actually my main guy
orlando id like you to meet dick

dick
mister hinkle

orlando
nice to meet you

mando
mister hinkle is an executive here at repropsych
orlando is my son

dick
oh
he works for you

orlando
its just tempor—

mando
yes
like i said
we run this business like a family

dick
smart man
keep that money in the family where it belongs

mando
its important to me to teach my son the value of a dollar
from behind **orlando** *we see a guy in a hoodie walking up*
he doesnt see **orlando**
its **sean**

sean
yo dad are you almost done
you said itd be fifteen minutes and its been a half hour
im fucking starving

dick
were wrapping up

> **sean** *and* **orlando** *see each other*

orlando
hey

> **sean** *is uncomfortable*

dick
armando this is my son

> **mando** *immediately sticks his hand out to shake* **seans** *hand*
> *he doesnt*
>> *more out of confusion than disrespect*

orlando
what are you doing here

dick
excuse me

sean
ummm

dick
do you two know each other

orlando
yea

sean
we go to school together

mando
its nice to meet a friend of orlandos

dick
you go to that fancy private school too huh

orlando
yes

dick
youre lucky your father is spending all that money on you

mando
yes
he doesnt realize
thats where it all goes

orlando
okay dad
i didnt even want to go there
you like forced me

dick
you get a scholarship
i havent seen a lot of latino kids there

orlando
what
no
of course not
my dad

mando
like i said
its an extravagance

dick
now i see where all my moneys going

sean
thats a weird uniform

orlando
its just—

                              sean *starts to laugh*

sean
are you a janitor
i thought you were all rich and shit

mando
a job is a job

sean
sorry i didnt mean any disrespect

orlando
i mean this isnt really my job

mando
were not rich

orlando
whatever
i had fun last night

dick
you saw each other last night
i thought—

mando
werent you on a date

orlando
dad shut up

dick
a date

mando
thats
wow
look at that
were doing business and our kids are going out
fate

sean
i wouldnt call it a date

orlando
okay
i mean we

mando
dont be embarrassed boys
we are very progressive
we support you
were here were queer

dick
youre dating a—

mando
hes not—

orlando
i dont really work here
this is a giant misunderstanding
im not a janitor
obviously
im the boss's son—

dick
sean
when i told you you could do better than becky—
you didnt tell me you were going out—

sean
we didnt really go out

orlando
except we did

sean
it wasnt a date
he had those concert tickets
remember
i begged you to buy them for me
for weeks i kept asking you get them for me
but you said they were too expensive
i had to do what i had to do

        dicks *face goes ice cold*
            hes humiliated
                  but hes trying not to show it
          but **mando** *can see it*
             he can see and feel all of it

orlando
i dont really work here
tell him dad
tell him
dad
why arent you saying anything

mando
orlando get inside
now
dick let me walk you to your car

orlando
dad

dick
were leaving
lets talk later

sean
i have to go to the bathroom

dick
hold it

mando
its okay
orlando show him to the bathroom

dick
HEY

> **dick** *starts to walk away*
> **mando** *goes after him*
> sean *starts to follow* **dick** *but* **orlando** *grabs him*
> **(the following underlined section is all overlapping dialogue)**

orlando
i thought we had a nice time
ive been thinking about you all day

sean
of course you were

mando
like i said
i really appreciate your business and look forward to continuing our long
fruitful partnership

dick
it appears
like i suspected
that were paying you too much

orlando
sean

> **orlando** *tries to kiss* **sean**
> **sean** *pushes him away*
> *its not violent but its not kind*

sean
stop

dick
sean
now

mando
you looked at the numbers
we went over them in detail
our prices are reasonable

dick
sean were leaving
do you hear me

orlando
okay
we had fun
ill call you later

mando
ill make some adjustments
and ill bring the contracts in to you personally
ill do what i need to make it work

dick
ill keep you posted

sean
dont
youre dirty dude
filthy

orlando
its just a uniform

sean
you stink
i can smell the shit on you

mando
what did you say to my son

dick
stay out of it
its not your fight to fight

silence and tension as everyone looks at each other

orlando
hes right dad

mando
orlando

orlando
dad
please

a moment

mando
youre right dick
this has nothing to do with us
let the kids sort out their own mess
we have business to wrap up
this partnership matters

dick
what partnership

orlando
fuck you

mando
orlando

sean
whoa

dick
what did you say

orlando
who the fuck do you think you are

dick
you better put a muzzle on your kid

mando
hey relax hes a kid
were the adults here

orlando
dont talk to him like that
sean
youd be lucky to have someone like me
you were born here
you were born here and you can barely read
im in ap english and you cant get past the first page of moby dick
this is your son
this is what you made
you should be so proud
my dad doesnt even have a high school diploma
and he has to bow his head down to you
why

were better than you
were better than you and youre mad because you know it
i didnt learn english until third grade
i know your own language better than you
and you think what
you think what

mando
orlando

orlando
how could you let this guy talk to you this way
dad
youre better than this
this

dick
come on sean
lets get out of here

orlando
what are you
whats even your title dude
you talk to my dad like youre on the same level
let me guess
supervisor
assistant to the vice president
some sort of middle-management position
obviously
thats so obvious

sean
thats not cool dude

orlando
you can tell by the way you speak
the way you are so desperate to prove yourself
the way you have nothing to show
the way you cant afford concert tickets
ha
you talk to my dad
a ceo
like youre on the same level

dick
you let your son talk to me that way

mando
im sorry
orlando

orlando
a chief executive officer
you know what that means
the one in charge
not some middle-management ant no one would miss
but you talk to my dad this way
why
your kid is barely getting through school

sean
hey

orlando
you think
fuck you
yea sean
youre hot
thats all you are
and you know what
you already peaked
this is the best youll ever be
from now on
for you
for you
look at your dad
thats the best youll ever be
if that
and thats not much—

                         mando *cuts* **orlando** *off*

mando
orlando

orlando
dad

mando
get inside

orlando
you deserve better than this
why dont you know that

dick *coolly looks at* **mando**

mando
orlando get back to work now

orlando
but dad

mando
AHORITA
andate para adentro
no lo creo
MY SON—

orlando *storms inside*

mando
please
this account
its fifty percent of my business

dick
thats not my problem
sean
get in the car

mando
i have a family
i have a son

dick
dont beg
its embarrassing

they go
and **mando** *just stands there*
broken

and like a shotgun we go inside . . .

sueños.

moments later

rafael *is cleaning an office*

orlando *storms in*

orlando
why dont you want to hang out with me

rafael
what

orlando
my dad said mercedes told him
he was happy we were hanging out

rafael
i told you
i came here to work

orlando
why dont you like me

rafael
i do like you

orlando
what are you afraid of

rafael
me
nothing

orlando
i ask you to talk to me
i ask you about yourself
i am a curious person
and i want to know
i want to talk to you
but you keep—

rafael
i am private
i am allowed to be private

orlando
okay
so ill just keep talking

im an open
im a very open person
i have a question for you
what do you think of this conundrum
do you know that word
conundrum
something ive been thinking about
they have this saying
in america
or maybe its just like a world saying
like everyone says it
i dont know

rafael
what saying

orlando
they say that girls fall in love with men that are like their father
men that remind them of their fathers
and so i always wonder
being gay
you know
does that mean that im going to fall in love with someone who is
    like my dad
or does it mean im going to fall in love with someone like my mom
like
what is the parallel you know
its something i wonder about a lot

rafael
orlando i dont know what youre talking about

orlando
i know what you are

rafael
what i am

orlando
and so i dont understand
why you are so
so
so
am i that
am i that disgusting to you

a moment

rafael
we arent alike

orlando
this again

rafael
escuchame
no somos igual
somos differente

orlando
por que

a breath

rafael
i am not brave like you
my father doesnt speak to me
he is ashamed
my mother
when we talk on the phone
all she does is cry
todo lo que tenia
lo perdi
ya no tengo sueños
estoy solo

orlando *kisses* **rafael**
hard
rafael *fights back*
for a second
but then he gives in
they kiss
is it beautiful?
is it sad?
is it scary?
they kiss
they kiss
they kiss
the door opens
mando *is there*
a moment
mando *is shocked*

                                        he seethes with rage
                    orlando *stands proud*
                                defiant
                                rafael *is panicked*

rafael
i didnt—
perdoname señor

                                    rafael *tries to run out the door*
                        mando *grabs him*
                                it is strong but not violent

mando
never show your face to me again

                                    he lets go of **rafael** *who runs out*
                            they stand there

orlando
the other day mom said
you know we dont mind that youre gay
but it would be nice if you dated a latino guy
that would make your father happy

mando
do not bring your mom into this

orlando
i just thought you should know

mando
por que sos como sos

orlando
i always wondered
why go to another country if youre not going to learn the language

mando
i didnt come here and work the way i have so you could end up with
someone like him

                            orlando
                                walks
                                    towards **mando**
                    they are very close

orlando
im glad you feel that way dad
now you know why i date white guys
i wanna marry up

and **orlando** *leaves*
his father in a state of shock

later

family.

> *sometime later*
> *the office*
> **mercedes** *is packing*
> *after a moment*
>
> **orlando** *walks in*
> **mercedes** *looks at him*

mercedes
your fathers not here

orlando
oh i know

mercedes
i didnt think you worked here anymore
dont tell me with all the layoffs
he actually needs you now

orlando
no thats—
of course not

> *THAT makes her pause*

mercedes
of course not
how could i be so crazy
to think

orlando
where will you go

mercedes
a small startup
its close to home

orlando
i cant believe he laid you off too
i thought at least you—

mercedes
is that what he told you—

orlando
i assumed

mercedes
well he didnt

orlando
oh
then why

mercedes
i quit

orlando
what

mercedes
i needed something different

orlando
but he was grooming you here
youre family

she pauses

mercedes
is there something i can do for you

orlando
how is he doing

mercedes
who

orlando
rafael

a breath

mercedes
hes fine

orlando
hes not answering his phone

mercedes
i dont know what to tell you

orlando
why did you tell him to stay away from me

mercedes
orlando
i have a lot of work to get done

orlando
i can help—

he goes to grab something

mercedes
dont touch that

orlando
im sorry

mercedes
no im sorry
i shouldnt have yelled at you like—

she takes another breath

orlando
i just dont understand why you would tell him that
i thought we were friends

mercedes
i was right wasnt i

this stings

orlando
youve known me since i was a kid
this warms her

mercedes
its not your fault
you dont know better

orlando
thats—
youre being condescending

mercedes
thats a big word

orlando
whatever
will you just pass along a message
for rafael

mercedes
you want to see him again

orlando
i just want to apologize
for what happened

mercedes
and what did happen

orlando
i dont know

mercedes
you dont

orlando
its private

mercedes
i see

orlando
just tell him im—

mercedes
you dont get it do you

orlando
get what

mercedes
hes missing
hes gone
he ran away

orlando
ill help you find—

mercedes
youve done enough

orlando
my dad can make some calls—

mercedes
your father
            she laughs

mercedes
he made it clear that if he ever saw his face again
he'd call la migra

orlando
he wouldnt
im sure he was just mad

mercedes
it doesnt matter
the threat was enough
and now
we dont know where he is

orlando
we can call around—

mercedes
theyve built this whole world around you
a bubble
a nice cocoon you can be safe in
its not like that for the rest of us

orlando
ill make him listen—

mercedes
make him
you cant make him do anything

orlando
im sorry

mercedes
dont say that

orlando
dont tell me what to do

she pauses

mercedes
i no longer work here
i have to remind myself
that after today
i never have to see you again
i dont work for you anymore—

orlando
you never worked for me—

mercedes
you would come here as a kid and play with the printer

you had homework
you needed to make copies from a book
who would do that for you
no matter what other work i had to do
who stopped to take care of it for you

orlando
i thought you enjoyed helping me

mercedes
you thought i enjoyed the extra work
you thought i enjoyed standing there turning one page than the next
hitting print over and over and over
for eighty pages
ninety pages
one hundred pages
you thought i liked to stay late afterwards to catch up what i hadnt
    finished
my actual work
instead of being with my family—

orlando
you could have said something

mercedes
you still believe that

orlando
its the truth

a breath

and then like a volcanic eruption

mercedes
the truth
the truth is youre an entitled brat
the truth is ive watched you grow and go from one of us
to one of them
the truth is i had to sit and grit my teeth
and be polite
because your father paid me
the truth is
i never have to bend backwards for you again
the truth is
i hoped you would be better than every asshole straight white guy that
ever looked at me like

i was just tits from another country
even though i was born here and have never even been to mexico
but instead
somehow
we turned you into one of them
the truth is
i expected more from you
i expected better
the truth is
i dont have to pretend anymore

orlando *starts to go*
he pauses
then he turns around

orlando
theres this guy at school
sean
hes everything i want
he doesnt have to work that hard and everyone wants to be around him
or be him
or do him
i thought that maybe i could have him
its foolish now to think
im sure you think
how could i be so
blind
so stupid
so
to think
i know where i belong
i do
im not crazy
dont think im crazy
but i guess i thought
i thought
dad always told me i could be whatever i wanted to be
to reach for the stars
i think i tricked myself into believing what he did
i think i tricked myself into seeing what he sees
i thought the money would help
at least that
would set me apart

but he didnt want me
of course he didnt
because
what am i
im not on his level
im beneath him
nothing
he doesnt need anything from me
and then
i didnt want rafael at first
he doesnt have money
hes a janitor
its not like i could date him and and and
what
we would go out
he cant afford dinners and concert tickets and nice presents
i like nice things
im sorry i do
he cant give me any of that
and if he met my friends
what would i say
this is my boyfriend
hes a janitor
i mean
its an honorable job
it is
i know that
it made my dad into something
but i already am something right
or thats what i thought
so rafael
he isnt right for me
he isnt
i feel gross saying it
he isnt good enough for me
hed be
like
i dont know
an investment
but after sean
i reached for the stars
i missed

i flew too high and my wings melted
i missed my dream
so i thought
maybe rafael
maybe i could give him the dream
me
but even him
my safety school
disappeared
even he
turned me down
if im not good enough for that
for him
he should be so lucky
he should be so lucky
dont you think
he should be so lucky to have someone like me
look at him
want him
but no
even he
and now
the money
it didnt
what do i have to offer anyone
if not that
if that wasnt enough
who am i
without it
what can i offer anyone
im just
worthless
im just—

mercedes
our jobs
your dads business
what he built
you cost us our lives for—

orlando
i wanted to matter

mercedes
congratulations big man
you matter
now what

she picks up a box and walks out

blackout

origin story.

> *months later*
> > *we are in front of a middle-class apartment building*
> **orlando** *comes out*
> > > *he sits*
> > > > *after a moment*
> > **mando** *comes out*

mando
you tired already

orlando
thats a lot of stairs

mando
its a good workout
im in better shape than you
punch my stomach

orlando
youre dumb dad
youre old
act your age

mando
im not the one sweating and tired

orlando
whatever

mando
do you like the apartment

orlando
its fine

mando
im sorry its so small

orlando
its fine dad

mando
but like i said
its only temporary

orlando
i understand

mando
you used to love this neighborhood
you said you missed it

orlando
havent lived here since i was seven dad
i dont remember it that much

mando
well you were happy here

orlando
if you say so

mando
its a good thing were downsizing now
youll go off to college soon and your mom and i will be alone
so this is coming at a good time
dont want too much space
a big empty house with only two people in it

orlando
yeah

mando
but when you come back to visit
well go and look at open houses
by then everything should be in order and well find something new
remember when we would spend the weekends going from open house to
    open house
your mom fell in love with every house we saw
every single one
i had to say no
not enough bedrooms
or the backyard is too small
or there isnt enough light
i had to be practical
but every time—

orlando
until you found the perfect home

mando
exactly

orlando
except its gone now

mando
its just a temporary setback

orlando
i know

> *a moment*
> *a gust of wind*
> *leaves blowing around them*

mando
im sorry you couldnt finish out your time at st nicks

orlando
i told you its fine
we dont have to keep talking about it

mando
i just want you to understand
the tuition money were saving on that private school
itll make a big difference for college
i want to give you as much as we can
dont want to saddle you with too many loans
debt

orlando
entiendo papa

> *leaves*
> *leaves*
> *leaves*

orlando
perdoname papi

> *a breath*

mando
you didnt do anything wrong
you did exactly what i would have wanted you to do
you know that right

> *a breath*

orlando
i like it here

mando
like i said
its only temporary

orlando
its okay dad
even if it isnt
ill get used to it

mando
i dont want you to get used to it
we did it once
well do it again
do you hear me

a moment

orlando
why
theres no point
i finally understand
that life
it was never meant to be for us
they made the rules so that we couldnt win
were dogs chasing our own tails for their enjoyment
and they wonder why were mad

mando
dont say that

orlando
dad
its easier this way
i promise
at least we know now

orlando *gets up*

orlando
coming

        mando *wants to say more*
            he wants to fight his son
                he wants to tell him hes wrong
       he wants to tell him that everything will be okay
           but for the first time in his life
                hes not sure

mando
en un momento
i want to enjoy the air

> **orlando** *goes inside*
mando *sits in silence*
> *he takes a deep breath*
> *he looks at the sun*
he takes another deep breath
and then another
and another
until a small sob comes out
he cries in a desperate
overwhelmingly loud silence
the sound of birds
the sound of birds

end of play.

the strangers

by christopher oscar peña

this ones for
> **bill heck**
>> *for all the sunrises*

>> *and*

for
> **arthur kopit**
>> *believing in young writers and opening doors for so*
>> *many of us*

The play was developed with generous support from the Lark Play Development Center (John Clinton Eisner, Artistic Director) at their annual residency with New York Stage and Film.

the strangers was originally commissioned and had its world premiere by the Clarence Brown Theatre (Cal MacLean, Artistic Director) in Knoxville, Tennessee. Opening night was Friday, February 23, 2017.

It was directed by John Sipes.

SCENIC DESIGN	Andrea Lauer
LIGHTING DESIGN	Kenton Ycager
COSTUME DESIGN	Andrea Lauer
SOUND DESIGN	Vincent Oliveri
PRODUCTION STAGE MANAGER	Caleb Cook

The cast was as follows:

CRIS	Aaron Orlov
DAVE	Jeffrey Dickamore
DIEGO/GUY2	Miguel A. Faña
SARAH/HOMELESS PERSON	Emily Kicklighter
ELEANOR/WG2/WEDDING PLANNER/ CAROLINE	Charlotte Munson
EMILY/WG1	Lauren Pennline
PEARL/CROSSING GUARD	Carlene Pochette
NIEGEL/GUY	Jude Vincent

note

this play fucks with Thornton Wilder's *Our Town*. in that case, this play can be called many things: a response to, an appropriation of, a remix, an adaptation, a counterpoint, an updating, who knows.

it is my intention that all of the actors in this play should play a set character, and then multiple smaller characters. it is up to the production and its director to figure out whether this means that the audience should not know, and that the actors are fully disappearing into each character, or if part of the theatrical language of this play is that the audience fully knows, and is aware of actors playing more than one role. also, everyone plays more than one role EXCEPT the actors playing dave and cris.

a note on design

in the original version of *Our Town*, we visited one town. it is my intention that the world of our play both be one town that cris be revisiting, and yet that that town be every town. and what i mean by that: this town is the town of america. yes, i know that new york city is as vastly different from santa barbara as it is from knoxville, as it is from tampa or minneaopolis or poughkeepsie. and yet as vastly different as we are politically and culturally in various pockets of america, there are still some shared values and landmarks. you can find mcdonald's and walmart anywhere. most places have gas stations, bridges, houses. so the landmarks, both physically and metaphorically of this play, should remind the audience that "our town" is the whole of modern america.

to this degree i think the set should be surreal and abstract, almost like a rubik's cube. i think it should constantly be reinventing itself as the play progresses. there should be hidden nooks and crannies. a window becomes a painting. a car becomes a piece of a monopoly set. maybe a character talks about a bridge thats very specifically the brooklyn bridge but in the background we see the red steel beams of the golden gate. im also interested in these ideas: how can the set sometimes feel like the universe from space, and then other times feel like weve zoomed into the thread of an old rug. play with magnification constantly zooming in and out. the micro is the macro is the micro is the macro. i am interested in the idea of physical, spatial, emotional, and metaphorical dissonance. take that for what it means to you.

characters

dave—the definition of all-american white guy, that one you always wanted

diego—latino guy, full of reckless abandon and hindered by short sightedness
also plays **guy2**

niegel—a young black male, the future
also plays **guy1**

emily—that white girl, you know the one, dont make me spell it out
also plays **wg1**

pearl—a black woman you think is from paris but is actually from a suburb
also plays the **crossing guard**

sarah—white girl. the. most. basic
also plays the **homeless person**

eleanor—white girl. your best friend. the one you love the most
also plays **wg2** and **caroline** and the **wedding planner**

and

cris—ethnically ambiguous. the one were trying to save

and

various wedding guests

the first act:

"living"

welcome.

> *the* **company** *makes their way out.*
> *they wave at people, maybe shake hands*

> *theyre warm*
> *inviting.*

dave
thank you for—

niegel
seriously dude

emily
told you he couldn't

dave
what

pearl
we talked about this

niegel
seriously

dave
im sorry i didnt mean to

diego
words man

niegel
you always gotta be the first voice in the room dont you

dave
i just
i get so excited

emily
youre like a puppy

niegel
thats one—

eleanor
you said you wouldnt do this

dave
i apologize okay
im sorry

diego
now we just look like a bunch of—

emily
can you not say anything—

pearl
there might be kids in the audience

sarah
oh i hope not

diego
amateur
okay
i was going to say amateur

pearl
oh well

emily
hes not wrong

diego
you guys are always expecting the worst from me
when hes the one—

pearl
alright then
we are here to welcome you

niegel
to say hello

emily
as a company

eleanor
yes a company
not in discord

pearl
not this early anyway

sarah
bienvenidos

niegel
is she serious

eleanor
you didnt

niegel
i mean
bro
can you believe this

sarah
what
its a nice word
i learned it in spanish class

diego
somebodys gonna have to handle this

sarah
what does that mean

pearl
but seriously

sarah
i was just trying to be inviting

diego
inviting
oh okay
so were doing like
what
like that ride
whats that ride called
with the kids and the people
and the boat
at disneyland

dave
oh man i love disneyland

niegel
okay but you know about disneyworld though right

eleanor
"its a small world after all"

diego
yea
that one

dave
i think what my buddy here is trying to say is—

niegel
dude
we talked about this
you dont have to speak for us

dave
im sorry

diego
i just
i mean
bienvenidos
okay
so did you
are you going to speak russian
and mandarin
maybe farsi and bengali too

sarah
no i just know the important ones

pearl
important ones

sarah
i mean
thats not what i meant

niegel
be clear

emily
words mean something

sarah
okay ill just stop talking

eleanor
thats not

pearl
we wanted to start off the evening by coming out as a company
and welcoming you to tonights
what did we decide on

sarah
play

niegel
it is
but i mean is it

dave
performance

diego
im really not

dave
what man

diego
i dont know it just feels
i dont know
like inauthentic or whatever

emily
experience
event
how about event

eleanor
how about story

niegel
yea i think

emily
sure

pearl
works for me

emily
The story you are about to see is called the strangers

dave
the author is christopher oscar peña

diego
a first-generation honduran-american playwright raised in california

diego
this piece is a response to

sarah
remix of

niegel
appropriation of

eleanor
our town by thorton wilder

sarah
considered one of the great american plays of the twentieth century

pearl
arguably

diego
if you know it
    congratulations

pearl
if you dont
    youll be fine

dave
this play our town premiered in 1938

emily
the strangers premiered
well
now

diego
we are grateful that you have come to share this story
this experience with us

eleanor
that you have given us your time

niegel
that which is
in a way
the most expensive

emily
that thing you cant get back
none of us can
no matter how hard we try

dave
and we just
i guess we wanted to welcome you into our home and
well
build community
so many of us are strangers
you know
and were hoping that when this is all over
maybe we wont be

sarah
yea

diego
i like that

eleanor
we also felt that we wanted you to hear from all of us tonight
together
but also individually

pearl
we wanted to put more voices in the room

eleanor
the ones that you probably hadn't heard before

niegel
or hadn't heard often
often enough

diego
we also thought it would feel more democratic

emily
yes

sarah
democratic
what does that mean

eleanor
well
government by the people
for the people
i think thats—

sarah
no i mean
i know what democracy is
i meant
in this context

diego
social equality

niegel
i think it means
it means—

eleanor
we all get to speak

sarah
oh
yea
of course
that makes sense

emily
so i think we can start now
at the very beginning

dave
well
i mean you could argue

eleanor
but were not

diego
dude does have a point
this could be the middle

niegel
or the beginning of the end

pearl
dont say that

dave
yea i take that back—

pearl
we cant always take things back

emily
its out there now

pearl
look
we are starting here
with us
with you
with them
with us
this is where we start
this is our beginning
cris comes home

eleanor
so
cris comes home

pearl
is he from here

dave
i guess it depends
on what you mean by home

emily
cris comes back

> *we see* **cris** *appear holding luggage*

dave
cris returns to a place he used to know

diego
but time has passed

niegel
time always does

eleanor
and things are different

sarah
things are different

pearl
to say the least

dave
cris returns to an unfamiliar place

pearl
we begin here

diego
welcome

niegel
welcome

eleanor
welcome

company
welcome

they vanish.

an echo.

> **cris** *stands in the space*
> > *he takes in a giant breath*
> > > *he stands in one place and looks out*
> > > > *in the distance*
> > > > > *the sound of*
> > > > *waves*
> > > > > *crashing.*

> *he turns around*
> > *he makes a circle*
> > > *he takes so much of it in*
> > > > *and then*
> > > > > *the sound of a voicemail*
> > > **cris** *plays the voicemail*
> > > *we do not see the speaker but instead hear her voice*
> > > > *the voice is his entire universe*

and fills up every particle of space
> *it is the voice of a latina woman*
> > *mom*

cris' mom
hijo
ya llege
finalmente
mi primer vuelo salio tarde entonces perdi el segundo
usted sabe como pasan estas cosas
esta ves solo nos perdieron dos bolsas
siempre lo mismo
pero por lo menos esta ves traje lo mas importante en mi mano
hijo mio
lo extraño mucho
mucho mucho mucho mucho mucho

> > > *a moment*
> > > > *she cant breathe*
> > > *she is crying*

hijo mio
i wish you was with me
i wish that you know how much i love you
i love you so so so so so so much there isnt enough room in the world
i wish you know that

please mijo
it is important to me
i wish that you come home
i wish you know where home was
i try
im sorry i could not help you
i wish that i had not given you such a big hole in your heart
i wish that you find what you are looking for
i wish you everything
when will i see you again—
and the voicemail cuts off

cris
mother made it back to honduras
home
a place i dont know

and then . . .

arrival.

niegel
an airport

> *the set reveals itself*
> *a welcome sign maybe*
> *or the carousel where luggage comes out*
> *tumbling out carrying various lives*
> *from*
> *every*
> *different*
> *place*

emily
wait i want to

niegel
you love this part

emily
i just
that moment you know
when two people meet
for the first time
that moment
possibility
the world before them

niegel
before they know

emily
hey

niegel
how it all turns out

emily
Niegel
what about

niegel
dont say it
i hate when you say this
its so

emily
what

niegel
optimistic

emily
sometimes the journey
is more important than the outcome

niegel
youll never change will you

emily
is that what you really want

                              a moment

niegel
cris arrives back to a place he used to know

emily
a guy appears

                              dave *appears*

niegel
he is in a car
nothing fancy

emily
kind of
the car is old

niegel
some would call it economic

emily
the guy has been tasked to pick up cris
and take him home
that was all

niegel

emily

emily

cris checks his phone
the two have never met

niegel
so he wants to do his research

                                        cris *checks his phone*

emily
research
come on
he wants to know if hes cute
wouldnt you

cris
basic

emily
WHAT

cris
i mean hes not ugly
he just
he looks like every other white guy youve seen a hundred times
i know he has good cheekbones but
whatever

emily
thats what you say now

niegel
emily

emily
okay okay
ill shut up

                                cris *and* **dave** *are in his car*

dave
cris

cris
dave

cris
thank you for doing this
i'm sure its such a drag to have to babysit me instead of enjoying your
    saturday

dave
please
were really excited to have you here

the company manager had a last-minute family thing
i was happy to volunteer

cris
thats
nice of you to say

dave
how was your flight

cris
long

dave
you went to college here

cris
its been a long time
nothing looks the same

dave
what would you like to do

cris
what

dave
they told me to pick you up
take you to where youre staying
stop off and grab food if you were hungry
you know
get you settled in
if you need to sleep
youre probably tired
so whatever you want
but i can also take you somewhere nicer to eat
i can show you around town
like i said whatever you want

emily
cris looks at dave

niegel
dave smiles

emily
his smile is warm
like an ocean you can get lost in

cris
are you sure you dont have other stuff to do
really
i feel bad i crashed your day

dave
they gave me the day off
id love to show you around

cris
id love that to
show me your version of this place
                    an instantly recognizable song comes on

niegel
they drive

dave
first stop
this is where youll be staying

cris
oh my god
i used to live across the street

dave
small world

cris
its pink now
i remember when it used to be blue
did this building always look this old
or was i just so happy to be here the world seemed brand new then

dave
youre on the third floor
they gave you a room with a view
its a mixed building

cris
mixed

dave
its one of those
buildings
you know
where

some are transient
college kids
some are visiting artists
and then others are people who have lived here forever

cris
the building has been like that for years

dave
come on
lets drop off your stuff

       cris *and* **dave** *get out of the car*

eleanor
sunrise
as the sun begins to peak out
awaking from her own slumber
a stranger arrives
meanwhile next door
a couple awakes

next door

modern-day romance.

>   *a young womans room*
>   *posters of super-cool pop punk performers*
>   *like miley if she had class*
>   *whatever the kids are listening to*
>   *and a vintage poster of an old play*
>   *the more we live in the future*
>   *the more we crave trinkets from the past*
>   *the poster is for an old play called "our town"*
>   *a black woman lies in a bed sleeping*
>   *wait*
>   *IS she sleeping?*
>   *her eyes are closed but then we notice*
>   *shes breathing hard*
>   *and as her breathing gets louder*
>   *her arms come up over her head*
>   *she grabs a pillow or a headboard and then we realize*
>   *oh snap*
>   *under the sheets*
>   *theres a mass moving vigorously between her legs*
>   *after a moment*
>   **pearl** *climaxes!*
>   *the mass comes out from under the sheets*
>   *a white girl appears*

emily
how was that

pearl
i cant breathe

emily
youre welcome

pearl
that was

emily
surprise

pearl
unexpected

emily
but good

it was good right
it was amazing
tell me it was amazing

pearl
it was amazing

emily
good
no ones ever complained

a moment

pearl
oh
you do this
all the time

emily
that wasn't
that isnt the point

pearl
you said it

emily
are you serious

pearl
what

emily
dont slut shame me

pearl
im not

emily
thats so like
last century of you
if i wanted someone slut shaming me id fuck a dude alright

pearl
thats not what i
dont be angry

emily
its just
i wanted
and now its ruined

pearl
what do you mean

emily
you told me
nothing
i cant do anything right

pearl
baby
dont say that
im sorry
sometimes i dont think when i say things
you know i get all awkward when people do nice things for me
i cant
i dont know why im like this

emily
you told me youve never woken up happy

pearl
. . . . . .

emily
. . . . . .

pearl
i shouldn't have

emily
. . . . . .

pearl
. . . . . .

emily
i thought maybe this way
i wanted to okay
i like being with you
love
being with you

pearl
emily

emily
and i thought to wake up in the
the

i dont know
throes of ecstasy
with the woman you love
care about
sorry

pearl
love

emily
yea

pearl
yea

emily
really

pearl
of course

emily
really

pearl
no doubt

emily
weve never

pearl
i know

emily
now i cant breathe

pearl
i love you

emily
i just thought if you woke up
feeling
you know
then

pearl
thank you

an alarm goes off

pearl
fuck
i have to get to class
we both do

emily
wait

pearl
you know i hate being late

emily
pearl

pearl
im sorry
we never have enough time

emily
i tricked you

pearl
what do you mean

emily
when you were sleeping
i changed your alarm

pearl
wait what

emily
i set it earlier than usual
so see
we have more time than you think

pearl
you stopped time for us
a magic trick

emily
you love it

                              they kiss

emily
so stay
just a little bit longer

pearl
okay

emily
tell me about your dreams

pearl
some people get bored with their lives
close their eyes
and see what they want
not me
my pain follows me wherever i go
it never lets me rest

emily
tell me

pearl
leave it alone

emily
i want to know

pearl
the dream is mine

emily
why wont you let me in
why wont you share
im trying to save you

pearl
im not yours to save

emily
fuck you

pearl
emily

emily
pearl

pearl
fine
you want to know what happens in the dream
i feel like im choking
theres never enough air
i wish for death

but it never comes
happy now

emily
no

pearl
i tried to spare you

emily
i was only trying

pearl
well stop

emily
im sorry

pearl
you dont have to apologize
its not your fault
its just
easier if you dont

emily
okay

pearl
i hate that i make you feel this way

emily
im fine
i love you

pearl
i love you too

a moment

emily
did you get the tubing by the way

pearl
yes
it came yesterday

emily
have you picked a day yet

pearl
i was thinking tonight

emily
i think thats a good idea
and your parents

pearl
theyre out of town
they dont know ill be there

emily
good
do you want me to come over and help

pearl
i think its best if you dont

emily
are you sure

pearl
i might stop myself if you do

emily
okay
you have to make sure everything is sealed okay
really sealed
otherwise not enough stays inside and it wont work
and im not just talking about your car doors
you have to make sure the sunroof is sealed
get lots of towels and put them under the garage door
anywhere there is a crack
people forget to do that

pearl
how do you know

emily
i went on a site
there was this one where people had messed it up
and so they have like all these techniques
just advice i guess on what they forgot to do

pearl
thats
helpful

emily
its called the hibachi method

pearl
what is

emily
when you kill yourself using carbon monoxide

pearl
why

emily
i dont know
i didnt get that far

the alarm clock goes off again
they both look at each other

pearl
now its actually time

they kiss

pearl
hey
isnt today your first day of rehearsal for our town

emily
that actor comes in today
the one playing the stage manager

pearl
cris something right

emily
i love his work so much
im really nervous

pearl
dont be
i know youre going to be amazing

emily
i wish you could be there

pearl
i know
me too

they kiss
and as they do
we zoom out

outside

on the streets.

cris *and* **dave** *appear*

dave
you have everything you need

cris
i think i do
just then **emily** *comes out of the apartment*

emily
dave

dave
emily
what are you doing here

emily
what nothing
i slept over at a friends
its none of your business
awkward breath

cris
hey

dave
sorry
cris this is emily
my sister

emily
its so nice to meet you
im a big fan

dave
cris is playing the stage manager

emily
DUH i know
i love that part
im playing emily
our parents named me after—

dave
im giving him a tour of the town today

cris
is this really a town

dave
what would you call it

cris
a pit stop

emily
remember to take him to the bridge

dave
thats a good idea
bye

emily
i gotta run
dont want to be late
nice meeting you cris
i cant wait to work with you

cris
absolutely me too

emily
bye

she goes
cris *looks at something*

dave
what

cris
that building there
what is it

dave
thats a cronut shop

cris
like croissant donut things

dave
exactly

cris
a whole shop dedicated to cronuts

dave
theyre delicious

cris
when i was here that was a copy shop
do you remember those

dave
no

cris
like a mom and pop kinkos
its where you got your textbooks copied
we had these things called readers
they were like collections of any articles you had to read for class made
      into a book
they were like forty or fifty dollars a piece because they were so
      enormous and you would have like
four or five in your bag depending on what classes you were taking
just stacks of copies and copies and copies

dave
oh
you mean a print shop
yea no
its all digital now

cris
they must have gone out of business
thats so sad

dave
why

cris
i had my first kiss in there

dave
while making copies

cris
it took so long
it was something to do while you waited
it seemed so romantic back then

a moment

cris
is that

dave
thats our local homeless lady

cris
oh wow shes still here

dave
shes been around that long

cris
oh god im old

dave
i didnt mean it that way

cris
i know
im kidding

dave
good
hungry

cris
starving

dave
know where you want go

cris
surprise me

dave
oh no
the pressure

cris
it better be good
im a judgmental bitch

dave
nah i bet youre not
you dont seem like the type

cris
give me a few hours

and as they go

home(less).

> *a* **homeless person** *approaches*
> > *they is very androgynous*
> *they take a seat on a bench*
> > > *their hands are cracked and their face is*
> > > *like a burnt piece of toast*
> > **homeless person** *loves it*
> > > *the sun*

homeless person
mind if i sit for a while
this is my favorite bench

they think i dont have a home but ive been here a lot longer than most of
them
this is all my home
this bench
that rock
that strip of concrete and that patch of shade
all of it
mine

ive been here so long ive seen kids come through
and then ive seen their kids and kids
they all think theyre so different
they so unique
like theyre discovering something new
like theyre christopher columbus and this is theirs now
but this place
it was here long before them
and it will be here long after them

the one thing ive learned
the music changes
the skirts get short and then they get long again and then they get shorter
the cars get upgrades
but the people
they all stay the same
that used to scare me

but now i realize
thats just life

all i see are a bunch of peope desperate to be heard
desperate to be seen
sometimes its in fashion to scream for what you want
and other times
you withhold
you hide
but in the end its all the same thing
hold my hand
be with me
love me

it sounds so simple to say that

people think the world should be about more

but it isnt
its just about that

do you see that spot over there
that building under construction
last year a boy got in his car
and killed a bunch of people

most people think hes a criminal
a monster
but i think he was just a sad sad sad boy
he wanted love and dint know how to get it
didnt know how to ask for it
so people thought he was weird

and what is weird anyway
except a new set of social norms that we follow for a certain period of
    time
people think im weird
but i know more than them
they just cant see

most people look
but they cant see

so this poor kid
ill tell you
he was gorgeous
like actually
he was a very good-looking boy
and he had money too
but no one taught him how to love

so he got in his car and left a note
saying
well
you can find it if you really want to

he got in his car and he drove down this street and he just ran people over
i remember seeing the bodies flying through the air

he came at top speed crashing into everything in his path until his car
    slammed into that storefront and exploded
up in flames

all that damage
all that death and destruction
all that pain
because no one taught him how to love

people come and go here
they leave their mark but they dont consider what that mark will do

they think theyre the first ones
the only ones

but thats not true
thats not true
im here to tell you that

im the historian of this place

even though i may not look it

anyway

the basics.

> *two* **white girls** *play soccer*
> *theyre warming up*
> *they play soccer during the exchange*
> *and by play soccer*
> *i mean they like pass the ball at each other*
> *semi-poorly*

wg1
so did you fuck him

wg2
what no

wg1
are you fucking serious

wg2
should i have

wg1
hes like the hottest guy youve ever gone out with

wg2
thats so mean

wg1
am i wrong

wg2
i mean

wg1
AM
I
WRONG

wg2
what about nathan

wg1
you mean the guy with the hairy back
we dont even call him nathan
we call him hairy back guy

wg2
but hes so nice

wg1

nice doesnt get likes on instagram

nice doesnt get you a big corporate job so mama can stay home and buy
   fendi

you know what nice gets you

a honda odyssey

have i taught you nothing

wg2

im sorry to disappoint you

god sometimes youre so right

wg1

the truth hurts

wg2

im trying to be better

wg1

did you at least suck his dick

wg2

. . . . . .

wg1

i cant with you right now

wg2

i gave him a hand job

wg1

what

wg2

i gave him a hand job

wg1

oh congratulations

the last time i gave someone a hand job i was fourteen years old

im so proud of you

wg2

i was

wg1

what

wg2

it was weird

wg1
weird how

wg2
he had
he was
he just had extra stuff

wg1
and

wg2
i didnt know what to do with it

wg1
you mean youve never seen an uncut dick before

wg2
all the guys ive been with are white

wg1
hes white

wg2
MIXED

wg1
okay mostly white

wg2
my dad would kill me

wg1
i didnt tell you to marry the guy
i said fuck him
not marry him

wg2
it freaked me out

wg1
. . . . . .

wg2
. . . . . .

wg1
look
were best friends
so i feel like its my duty to tell you this

wg2
okay

wg1
you remember that shakespeare play we read

wg2
which one

wg1
much ado about something i think

wg2
i didnt understand that one

wg1
nobody did

wg2
what about it

wg1
well theres this scene where this one guy wants this girl
and hes like desperately in love with her
and like the girl keeps rejecting him over and over and over
and everyones like what the fuck bitch
because
well HER best friend
eventually pulls her aside and says
and says
something like
basically know when to sell

wg2
i dont understand

wg1
basically bitch was like
girl you are a four and he is a seven
youre never gonna get dick like that again

wg2
okay

wg1
okay

wg2
okay

wg1
get it

wg2
i think so

> *another white girl, number three also known as* **sarah**, *rolls in*

sarah
fuck

FUCK
fuck fuck fuck fuck

wg1
what sarah

sarah
got my letter back from state

wg2
did you get in
you got in
congratulations

> **sarah** *throws severe shade at* **wg2**

wg1
dont be so dense
does it sound like she got in

sarah
you can be so basic sometimes

wg2
well
im sure there was some sort of mistake

wg1
yea
maybe they mixed up your paperwork

sarah
i didnt even get wait listed

wg1
that makes no sense

sarah
its where my mom and dad met
its where my older brother goes
its my
my
its my legacy
its my fucking right

wg1
absolutely

wg2
nothing has ever been more true

sarah
do you know
                    she pauses and looks around
huddle up
                    the girls huddle up
do yo know who got in

wg2
who

wg1
yea who

sarah
martha

wg1
wait what

sarah
martha with the hair

wg2
but shes

wg1
but shes

sarah
yea

wg2
but why

sarah
i had joanie pull up her grades

wg2
the counselor

sarah
yea

wg2
but how
isnt that like
i dont know
confidential

sarah
my mom and her are like best friends from like childhood
they go way back
like since before we born

wg1
that is back
like ancient times

wg2
damn sarah
you are so lit

sarah
dont say that

wg1
so what did you find out

sarah
we basically have the exact same grades

wg2
im so confused

wg1
yea
youre on the soccer team
and like have been class vp and president
and most importantly

everyone loves you the most
so like i dont
this makes no sense

sarah
its because shes mexican

wg1
what

wg2
i thought she was cuban

wg1
same thing

sarah
whatever
its because they dont usually get in
its because most of them can barely read
i mean look at our class
basically every mexican we grew up with has dropped out
theres that one who works at the costco

wg1
oh yea i remember him

sarah
and didnt like three of them get pregnant

wg2
they all get pregnant

sarah
so shes basically like last man standing
shes got like no competition so they like let her in

wg1
thats like racist
thats like so fucking racist

wg2
that bitch stole your spot

sarah
yea
she took it
she took what was mine

wg1
what are we going to do about it

wg2
you should sue

wg1
yea you should sue
can you sue

wg2
my dads a lawyer
you can sue for anything

wg1
yea
people should know
people should know these things are happening to us
its not fair

wg2
yea its not right its not right at all

sarah
wait look
there she is

>   *a latina walks by*

>   *they all stare her down*

>   *like a white chola gang*

wg1
what a bitch

wg2
how dare she look over here

sarah
fucking criminal

>   *a whistle rings*

sarah
fuck

wg1
leave it all on the field tonight boo
were with you

wg2
yea were with you

> **sarah** *and* **wg1** *run off*
>> **wg2** *just stands there*
> *then*

wg2
wait
AM I THE FOUR?
oh my god
im the four

transition.

the street
    a **crossing guard**
cris *and* **dave** *are about to cross the street*
the **crossing guard** *blows her whistle*
and raises a large STOP sign

cris *and* **dave** *cross the street*

dave
beautiful day right

crossing guard
rain or shine
everyday i wake up with breath in my lungs and sight in my eyes
is a good day

dave
she always says that

crossing guard
its the truth

dave
this is chris
hes visiting

crossing guard
welcome home

cris
how did you know

crossing guard
home is where the heart is baby

cris
i wish it was that easy

crossing guard
it is if you want it to be
were alive baby
WERE ALIVE

dave
have a good day

crossing guard
you know i always do

cris
see you around

crossing guard
i hope so

they cross the street
the **crossing guard** *blows her whistle*

crossing guard
this is something i wonder about
safety

let me rephrase that
something i wonder about is
do people ever really truly feel safe

actually
what i really wonder is
when did people
we as individuals
when did we stop feeling safe

when was feeling unsafe
so a part of our dna
so a part of who we are
so internalized that we no longer even realize it
that feeling unsafe is just the way it is
guy1 *walks by*

guy1
damn you got nice legs

he keeps walking

crossing guard
something i wonder about is
what is it like to be the kind of person whos never known what its like to
    feel unsafe
the constant fear of death

see back in the day
people used to leave their doors unlocked
or so i hear

back in the day
people used to say hi to their neighbors
now
you cant ever really know who to trust

black men get shot on the streets
a daily occurrence
cops are being murdered
not a daily occurrence
not yet anyway
and that makes me wonder
who is accountable

straight men kill gay men
gay men kill other gay men
gay men take their own lives

                              guy2 walks by

guy2
damn girl you want me to stop
ill stop for you any day of the week

crossing guard
what did you say

guy2
i said
even under all those clothes i can tell youre hot

crossing guard
dont talk to me that way

guy2
whatd you say bitch

                        a long
                              uncomfortable
                                    terrifying moment
                        until

learn to take a compliment

                        he goes
                              she is shaken

crossing guard
sorry

where was i
a muslim gets kicked off a plane
just because
an immigrant gets beaten on the streets
why not

i have a friend

a straight white guy
he asks me
what can i do
how can i help

he represents everything that is wrong with the world
but i understand
its not his fault
not actually
not him specifically

but i cant feel bad for him
i dont have the time for it
i dont have the energy
ive been feeling too much pain for other people
for myself
to feel bad for him

he says help me
he says i want to learn
i feel bad

i feel bad

and i just think
feeling bad
will never be the same as fearing for your life
every day
a fear so large

a trauma so inherent
you cant help but smile

i wake up and i smile
ive survived another day

who knows if this may be my last

she walks away

eleanor
i love her
i should tell you
a year from now a woman will have just found out her husband lost his
    job
already living paycheck to paycheck the news will be devastating
as ash shes driving
consumed in her fearful thoughts
the women will run this top sign

at that moment a young girl will be crossing the street
in a split second
the crossing guard jumps in front of the car
saving the girl
the crossing guard will be rushed to the hospital but will die later
    that night
but
beloved by all
the local park will be renamed for her
a little piece of land in her honor

date night.

> *outside*
> *a pavilion or courtyard*
> *a big water fountain built last year that looks like its from italy or greece*
> *a starbucks and an olive garden*
> *trees lots of trees*
> *the sound of laughter*
> *kids out with their parents*
> *single ladies having girls night*
> *the sound of clinks as people cheers*
> *couples on first dates*
> *the sound of possibility*

pearl
the sound of possibility

eleanor
what does that sound like
if you could imagine

pearl
what would that be
picture it

eleanor
well give you a second

pearl
a deep breath maybe

eleanor
a smiths song

pearl
that cannot be what you think of when you think of possibility
theyre so sad
thats more like
the end

eleanor
but when something ends
something new begins
its all about perspective

pearl
i guess thats true

eleanor
every day
you go for a walk
and you run into someone jogging

pearl
or you go to a restaurant and there are two people next to you

eleanor
or maybe here
now
look around you
all these people
out tonight
they all started somewhere

pearl
these relationships
will they last

eleanor
were in a bar

pearl
a restaurant actually

eleanor
really

pearl
the bar comes next
hopefully
but for now
were at a restaurant

eleanor
but they are drinking right

pearl
yes
there are drinks

eleanor
it just
you know
speeds things up

pearl
you make a good point

eleanor
thank you
there is dinner
there are drinks
and they sit outside

pearl
it is early yet
the sun still casts her glow

cris
i didnt know if it was a date
i mean
sorry
i was certain it wasn't a date
but i was confused
it felt
never mind

pearl
they sit together in the middle of a meal

eleanor
where so much of lifes great moments happen

pearl
we think so anyway

dave
you havent touched your truffle fries

cris
theres just so much food

dave
i feel like i made a poor choice
i feel like youre unhappy with my decision

cris
no really
no
everything is so good
im just slightly overwhelmed by all the choices

dave
i cant believe
no never mind

he laughs

cris
what

dave
its just
we just met
this is our first meal together
and were sharing food
people dont usually do that right

cris
well my herpes cleared up so you dont have anything to worry about

dave
i wonder if we have the same strain

they laugh

cris
i dont know i guess
yea i dont share food with people i just met
theres something
intimate about it maybe
but you wanted the burger
and i wanted the burger
and you wanted the chicken
and i wanted the chicken
why cant we have both right

dave
no no i agree
its just people arent normally like this
never mind
ive had one beer and i have no idea what im saying
anyway dont stop
tell me more about your family
so your brother diego is here
and your other brother is in south america
do you at least get along with him

cris
well

he and i have a very problematic relationship
if you can even call it that
i mean hes
so like
okay my parents are from central america
born and raised
and my dad is fair skinned and my mom is brown
like brown as fuck
and they both have accents
and im like this fair-skinned white kid with no accent
so people always think my mom is like my maid or whatever
you know that whole thing about being the black sheep of the family
they call me the white sheep

dave
thats funny

cris
anyway so my family was poor and then when i was in high school they
    became
well they made a lot of money
selling drugs obviously

dave
seriously

cris
no
NO
obviously no

cris
they made all this money
legally
they like drive jaguars and own like five houses like serious money
and so thats who i am
like im an overeducated kid who had no money and then had a lot but is
    like
aware of his privilege
but my little brother
he like went to college and dicked around and then graduated
hes i dont know
twenty-seven now
and hes never had a job
and for the last three years hes lived in a tree in south america

not like a treehouse
he like climbs a tree and like goes to the biggest branch and ties himself
    to it
like in the fucking hunger games or something because hes like i dont
    know
finding himself or whatever
he said i forgot my roots
he said i dont know where i come from
his facebook name is the name of an indigenous mayan god
meanwhile im like im like
we were born here you fuck
basically i just feel that like

he can behave this way
like hes poor
because he has the privilege to do so
our parents will do whatever for him
so i actually find that sort of insulting
he thinks hes like
with the people
but like is he really
and anyway
i say that because even though he has no accent
hes incredibly dark skinned
so maybe like he behaves this way because we walk through the world in
    very different ways
i dont know
its all very complicated
we havent really spoken in like two years

a moment

dave *just looks at* **cris**

dave
i was fascinated by him

cris
what
im so sorry
this is so embarrassing
we just met
i dont know why i told you all that stuff

dave
hey

dave *reaches over and touches* **cris'** *arm*
                              its incredibly tender

cris
i remember he made contact
his hand on my arm
and i remember thinking
why am i so good on dates with straight guys
but i can never get a gay man to fall in love with me
what do i do differently
his hand on my arm
i remember thinking
this is the best date ive ever been on that isnt a date

dave
hey

cris
im sorry
its stupid

dave
no
you should talk to him
you should talk to both your brothers

cris
are you serious
youre on his side

dave
no
no
im not saying that
im just
i want you to be happy

                              a moment

eleanor
and then the server comes out

pearl
and the moment is broken

niegel
im sorry you guys

i didnt know
everyone is so mad at me about this
but i was only doing my job

eleanor
we know

pearl
we get it

eleanor
sometimes you just lack intuition

pearl
like read a moment you know

niegel
whatever

> **niegel** *turns to* **cris** *and* **dave** *as he becomes the server*

niegel
can i get you another beer

dave
ah
what do you think

cris
we can do whatever you want

dave
we could get another beer here or go somewhere else

cris
or we could do both

dave
yea
okay
lets do both

niegel
the same thing

cris
yea thatd be great

dave
same

cris
i love this place

dave
i was so worried you wouldnt like it

cris
i thought you were going to take me to the cheesecake factory

we see a cheesecake factory in the distance

dave
seriously

cris
my parents love it there
we could be in new york or san francisco or santa barbara or
chicago
it doesnt matter
theyre always going to the cheesecake factory

dave
but i thought they had so much money

cris
i know
you cant buy people taste
i think
i think they love it because no matter where you go
a cheesecake factory will always look
sound
and taste the same
itll always feel like home

dave
but its so
homogenized

cris
i have this theory
that cheesecake factory is like actually
the perfect american metaphor

dave
how so

cris
theyre all the same no matter where you go
and the menu is like
i can have pizza today
or i can have some sushi if im feeling a little exciting
maybe ill get some tacos from mexico
or if im really living dangerously ill get some indian samosas
its like the most worldly menu
and yet
its the most whitebred interpretation of everything
thats where we live

dave
my ex-boyfriend

niegel
a record scratch

eleanor
a record scratch

pearl
a record scratch

cris
WHAT
but hes so

pearl
i know baby

cris
and i dont know what to say

eleanor
because even the ones who know better
who know they shouldn't be making assumptions
do

dave
my ex boyfriend used to love that place

the beers arrive

cris
cheers

dave
cheers

emily
eleanor i think youre going to be late

eleanor
oh shit
shes right

> **eleanor** *moves to another scene*

netflix and chill.

> **caroline** *and* **diego** *sit on a couch making out*

emily
caroline and diego
their love is real
twenty-three years from now their child will lead a revolution
big things come from small beginnings
but they dont know that now

> *the door to the apartment opens*
> **niegel** *walks in*

niegel
you guys ready

> *they keep at it*

ive been working all day
i smell like sweat and regreat
and fried oil
let me spray some cologne on real quick so i dont repel the ladies and
    then well get going
okay

> *he exits*
> *they keep at it*

niegel
alright lets do this
YOU GUYS

> *they break away giggling*

caroline
what

niegel
i dont want to be late

diego
man what are you talking about

niegel
the rally
in the plaza
people are gathering there in a few minutes

diego
thats cool

caroline
have fun

niegel
you said you would come with me

caroline
whats this one for

niegel
one what

caroline
rally

niegel
dont play with me

caroline
theres just always a rally

diego
its for that black kid that got shot down by the bridge

niegel
he had a name
we all have names

diego
i know bro

niegel
you guys
seriously
you said you would come with me

diego
when

niegel
last night

diego
you mean when we were drunk

caroline
that definitely does not count
i dont remember that

niegel
we werent that drunk

diego
says who
says you
man thats like being rufied into a promise

caroline
that shits not funny babe

diego
oh THATS not funny
okay

caroline
im trying to be a better feminist

           diego *grabs her tit*

diego
i like when you get all feminazi

niegel
you guys are being dicks

caroline
im tired
i kind of just want to stay in tonight

diego
yea babe
lets just netflix and chill

niegel
yo
you guys are my best friends
how you not gonna come out and support me

diego
dont question my loyalty
fuck you dude
we do support you

niegel
doesnt feel like it

diego
just cuz we dont support you in the way you want
doesnt mean we dont support you

caroline
agreed
rallies just arent our thing

niegel
your thing

caroline
come on niegel
dont be like that
if you want to rally
if you want to make signs and scream your lungs out
thats fine
thats your prerogative
but i just dont think
i just dont think thats actually very
i dont think it does much besides make more people angry
i believe in the system

niegel
the system is corrupt

caroline
so go in and change it

diego
besides im not trying to get into this whole anti-cop thing
i just dont dig it

niegel
you think that kid deserved to get killed

diego
dont put words in my mouth

niegel
then

diego
i heard he had coke on him

niegel
so

diego
im just saying

niegel
im pretty sure ive seen you rail a few lines here and then

diego
dont get me wrong
i love me a little yay yo
might do some tonight
but you dont see me running from the cops

niegel
thats cuz cops arent stopping you

diego
he resisted arrest

niegel
so he deserved to die

diego
listen
if youre a black guy and you know people are up your ass
maybe dont carry coke on you
carrying coke
thats his bad
its against the law
thats just fact
mistake one
okay he gets pulled over by cops
cops find the coke
okay apologize and take your punishment
nah
takes off running
mistake two
he put himself in that situation
he the one breaking all the rules so i gotta take my night off and
    go protest
what
his right to be an idiot

niegel
his right to live

diego
its not that complicated

niegel
how do you not see that it is
IT IS

diego
you know who hates the cops
people who have reason to
you stay out of trouble you stay clean
you all good
right babe

caroline
i mean
do i agree that he broke the law
yes
do i think he made it harder on himself
yes
do i think its okay he had a target on his back from the beginning
no

niegel
so then

caroline
like i said
i just dont think a protest helps
it just antagonizes people
there has to be another way
a peaceful way

niegel
we are getting killed off
there is no more time for peace
if we keep waiting like you want us to
there wont be enough of us left to fight back

diego
i love you man
lets agree to disagree

niegel
i dont think this is one of those things where we can afford to do that
    diego

diego
bro
im brown
you dont see shit happening to me do you

niegel
its not the same thing

diego
were all outsiders bro
neither of us is white
you know how people stare at me when i go out with caroline
the hatred
i get it
its real
but i keep my head down
and i keep moving
moving
moving

niegel
youre telling me im in this alone

diego
im telling you
this isnt my battle

caroline
diego

niegel
no its alright
i see
you know
you dont see it now
but after theyre done with us
theyre going to come for you too

niegel *leaves*

caroline
diego

diego
thats not
thats not what i meant

caroline
then what did you mean

diego
. . . . . .

caroline
diego
what did you mean

diego
im just tired okay
im just tired

> *a moment*
> > *they stare at each other*
> *hes pleading for her*
> > > *she shakes her head in utter disappointment*
> > *she grabs her shit and goes*
> > > > *the sound of a door slamming!*

bffs.

emily *and* **sarah**

sarah
you got in

emily
what

sarah
you didnt tell me you got in

emily
how did you know

sarah
everyones talking about it
how could you not tell me

emily
you seemed so disappointed about not getting in
i didnt want to make you feel bad

sarah
fuck you
i wouldnt feel bad
youre my friend

emily
yea
okay

sarah
youre not going are you

emily
why wouldnt i go

sarah
because of pearl
because of your girlfriend
she stayed here
she stayed here for you
she stayed in the town that she grew up in
to be with you
or did you forget that

emily
im not going to let a relationship dictate my whole life
i have things to do

sarah
youre so selfish

emily
besides pearls not like you

sarah
what does that mean

emily
pearl wants me to succeed
pearl wants me to be the best version of myself

sarah
what are you implying

emily
i wasn't implying anything
i thought i was being clear
youve peaked sarah
for the rest of your life
youll know
the best already happened to you

sarah
. . . . . .

emily
im going to be late for rehearsal

the night sky.

diego
if you could know the date that you were meant to die
would you want to know it?

niegel
would you live your life differently?

diego
i would
i would want to know
it would free me

niegel
i dont
every day
would be a countdown

diego
every day is a countdown

niegel
thats one morbid way of looking at it

diego
heres what we all know
this moment
right here
this moment could be your last
it could be the end of things
something

niegel
or it could be the beginning
every moment is an opportunity for something new

diego
anyway
it is the end of the day

niegel
above us
the night sky

diego
in one part of the world a young woman sits in her car

pearl *appears*

> *he sits in her car*

niegel
in another part of the world
two boys

diego
two men

niegel
two men
get to know each other

diego
discover each other

> *for the rest of the scene the night continues to darken*
> > *first the entire set becomes the stars*
> *the ceiling*
> *the floor*
> *the seats*
> > *the audience*
> > *the people*
> > > *all we see are stars*
> *WE ARE ALL STARS*
> > > *and then after a while*
> > > *the entire space becomes the universe*
> *the milky way*
> > *the aurora borealis*

> > > *and at the end*
> > > > *it will just be black*
> > > > > *pitch black*
> > *and all we will hear are their voices in the pitch-black universe*

cris
wait so south pacific
being in that show is what made you most proud
i am judging you
i am full of judgment

dave
wait

no
you dont understand

cris
and here i thought you were so cool

dave
hey
wait

cris
waiting

dave
you dont understand
my dad was a lieutenant in the war
and he doesnt
we dont have the best relationship
here youll appreciate this
so when i was a kid
my dad was a pilot
and okay
so this is true and really fucked-up

cris
i like true and fucked-up

> **pearl** *turns on the car*
> *she sits in it as carbon monoxide slowly fills her space*

dave
my father was an airline pilot and he would take me with him all the time

cris
thats awesome
so you were like always traveling

dave
i was his wingman
literally and figuratively
he would take me with him to hotel bars and basically use me to pick up
    women

cris
WHAT
how old were you

dave
as early as six as late as thirteen

cris
im not sure if thats horrible or amazing

dave
well
i havent really told you the horrible part

cris
i wait with bated breath

dave
my dad was still married
to my mom

cris
WHAT

dave
so like i would travel with him and he would pick up women and then i
    would come home with him
to my mom
and i would have this terrible secret

cris
this is maybe the most fucked-up thing ive ever heard

dave
i know

cris
and you didnt tell your mom

dave
how could i

cris
but like trust
and loyalty
and like
thats your mom

dave
but i didnt want to be the one to break her heart

cris
fucking hearts

dave
fucking hearts is right
so anyway
this went on for years
and eventually he married two of them in other states

cris
fuck the what

dave
right

cris
did he have other kids

dave
no
thankfully
not with the other women

cris
this is like a lifetime movie waiting to happen

dave
so anyway when i got into junior high
my dad
well he sort of figure out that i was gay

cris
oh

dave
and he
i mean i dont want to make a big deal out of it
it was a long time ago
but he basically beat me

cris
im so sorry

dave
well hes the one who ended up being sorry
i not only told my mom about the other wives
i called all the other wives and basically told them too

cris
oh fuck
oh fuck

all the fucks
you like
you like

dave
blew up his life

cris
thats kind of amazing
i mean horrible
but like kind of epic amazing

dave
so for obvious reasons we didnt speak for many many years
many years
not until i turned thirty actually

cris
wow
im sorry

dave
its okay

cris
so you guys are cool now

dave
we talk
a little

cris
wait how does south pacific play into this
that shit is so racist

dave
well yea
i know it is
but i was in a touring production
and i was playing this colonel
and it came to his town
and he came
and he was so proud of me
because here was his son in the uniform

cris
it was make-believe

dave
i know
but he saw what he wanted to
we took pictures

cris
of his gay son in a musical theater production
which is literally the gayest thing possible
musical theater
you were like on stage screaming homo homo homo

dave
i know
but it didnt matter
we see what we want to see i guess

>   *a moment*
>   **pearl** *starts to cough*
>   *her coughing gets louder and louder*

cris
all i see are the stars

dave
what about you

cris
what about me

dave
are your parents cool with you being gay

cris
my moms biggest problem with me is that im single

dave
oh
thats nice

cris
she thinks im lost
she thinks im searching for something
she thinks ive lost my way home

dave
have you

cris
how can you lose something youre not sure you actually ever had

> *pearls hacking cough gets worse*
> *she gets out of the car*
> *she dials her cell phone*
> *it rings*

> *elsewhere*
> *a ringing phone leads us to* **emily**
> *she answers*

emily
i thought you were doing it

pearl
i am
i was

emily
when

pearl
now

emily
then why

pearl
i was in the car and i just
i got scared

> *she coughs*

emily
where are you

pearl
im drowsy
so sleepy
its surprising
you'd think you'd be coughing or a burning
but no
its so gentle
im scared emily

emily
pearl
listen to me
you cant think about it
you just have to do it
you said you were gonna do it
like i dont get why you arent

pearl
i dont get it either
i dont know

emily
so i guess you arent gonna do it then
all that for nothing
im just confused

pearl
i dont get it either
i dont know
i am going to eventually

emily
no youre not pearl
this is it
you kept pushing it off saying youll do it
but you never do
its always going to be that way unless you take action now
and follow through
youll just make it harder on yourself if you keep pushing it off
you just have to do it

pearl
i do want to but
im like freaking out for my family

emily
i told you
ill take care of them
everyone will take care of them to make sure they wont be alone
and people will help them get through it
we talked about this and they will be okay and accept it
people who commit suicide dont think this much
they just do it

pearl
i know i know
thinking just drives me more crazy

emily
you just need to do it pearl
or im gonna get you help
you cant keep doing this every day

pearl
okay im getting back in the car

emily
you promise

pearl
i promise babe
i have to now

emily
like right now
you cant break a promise

pearl
i love you

emily
sweet dreams pearl

> **pearl** *gets back in the car*

cris
dave
youre disappearing
i cant see you anymore

dave
here

cris
what

dave
take my hand

> *they hold hands*

cris
hi

dave
hi

cris
this is

dave
shhhh

cris
. . . . . .

dave
im going to put my arm around you
is this okay

cris
i can hear you breathing

dave
its just you and me
floating together in the dark
its like were the only two people in the universe

cris
this

dave
what

cris
this is home

                                    they kiss

end of act one.

INTERMISSION

the second act:

"settling"

not for me.

the **ensemble** *re-enters the space*
> *maybe they are individually checking in on the audience members*
telling them its time to go to their seats
> *wondering if they had a nice stretch*
asking them where theyre from and was the drive here nice
> > > *connecting.*
> > *as much as one can in these circumstances*

> **cris** *surveys the audience and then after a moment*
> > *he makes a choice*
> > *he whispers his choice into the ears of the* **ensemble**
some are surprised
> *some are resistant*
> > *they all acquiesce*

> > > *maybe they all leave*
> > > > *maybe they sit in the audience*
> > > > > *with the audience*
> > > *and listen*

> > > > *its just cris and the audience now*
> > > > > *he wrings his hands*
> > > > *and then he thinks*
> > > > > *i dont wring my hands*
> > > > *he shakes them out*
> > > *hes not the kind of person who does that either*
> *he smiles*
> > *awkwardly*
> > > *to himself*
> *and to all of them*
> > > *but hes decided*
> > *hes going to be honest*
> > > *and theres no stopping him*

cris
uhm
so uhm

ive asked everyone if i could
from here on out
i know this is a bit unconventional
changing the uh
rules
but

> *he takes in a deep breath*
> *hes terrified*
> *he smiles*
> *hes terrified but this is*
> *this is the right thing to do*

i never thought i would get married
i didnt really think that marriage was for me

> *a moment*

at the time of her death

> *a breath*

my mothers biggest problem
no
not problem
my mothers biggest
concern
was that i wouldnt ever get married
that
i would be alone
i tried to explain to her that i was never really alone
that i had a lot of friends
that just because i wasn't seeing one person exclusively didnt mean i
    wasn't seeing many people
not exclusively
i was very honest with my mother
mostly
my mother was this incredibly strict third world
(my phrasing not hers)
latina
she believed in god above all things
i think
i mean she believed in god
she was catholic
so
she believed that you shouldn't have more than one sexual partner
that drinking was evil and tattoos were for gang leaders

drug dealers and rapists
she believed that a man should be with a woman
although to be fair
im not sure how much of that is the catholic thing
or the third world country thing
although down there
i mean are things really all that separate
i mean theyre barely separate here
anyway
so she believed in god
and all the rules that come with that
and she believed in julio Iglesias
song plays
that song comes on and all of a sudden
i'm a kid again
and i feel safe with her
my mother
the thing about my mother is
was
is
she loved so so so so much
she loved with all her heart
but the thing she loved most in the world was me
so she came here
this one thing
this one person
this tiny honduran woman
an immigrant who didnt speak english
and eventually
she transformed
i didnt know my mother knew magic
but its clear that she did
she was magic
when she found out i got a tattoo
after the initial shock
she decided that maybe
she decided some could be beautiful and maybe she should get one too
when i started listening to celine dion and mariah carey and the
    backstreet boys
she insisted they were her favorites as well and therefore we had to go to
    all the concerts together
when she found out i was gay

well she figured god didnt always know what he was talking about
thats who my mom was
i think at a very young age i was incredibly spoiled because
the truth is
no one was ever going to love me as much as she did
no one is
is
is
not ever
so in a way everyone ive met since
since my mom
since my whole life
is always operating at a deficit
no one was ever going to see me the way she did

when marriage equality passed my mom was the first person to text me
she was so happy
great i thought
what will i do now
now that i dont have that excuse
how can you tell your mother no ones ever wanted you

the truth is
i had sort of forgotten that
i wasn't think about marriage equality
or the law
i know its incredibly selfish to admit that
but i just
i didnt think it would ever apply to me

okay i know
you think im being hyperbolic
you think im being dramatic
but im not
i just didnt
its not like i thought about it all the time that way
marriage
its that instead
i didnt think about it at all
it stopped being a part of my life
my
consciousness

do you ever stand in front of the mirror and just stare at yourself

and try to make sense of
whats there
do you ever wonder if what you see and what other people see ever
i dont know
align
are there things that we all respond to in just the same way
or are we constantly in disagreement
in disaccord
being different is good i think
but
its like
okay

people tell me they love me all the time
but when i stand in front of the mirror
all i see is
all i see is
                    he cant even say it
its funny isnt it
that dissonance
dissonance

discord
cacophony
incongruity
inharmonious

i am inharmonious
when i realized that no one would ever love me the way i needed
    to be loved
the way i wanted to be loved
the way other people get to be loved
                a moment
the world is fucked-up
this is a true statement
the world is fucked-up

my mind is constantly
i think of rape and how many people i know have been
its horrifying
when you think of the number
theyre
crippling
and so of course like if youre a woman

how much of that fear is just so everyday that its like internalized its
    like
your dna
so much a part of you that you dont even have to think about it
    anymore

i think of the women in this room
most who have probably never even vocalized it

i think of all the people of color being killed
people of color
what a stupid phrase
i think of all the black men getting killed
unarmed men being murdered by people that are supposed to protect
    them

and then i think of all those horrible cops and how they've ruined it for
    all the good ones
there are good cops
there are
we know this
but when they all look the same
who can tell the difference

and then the latinos
no one talks about the latinos being killed
and how people hate immigrants even though
even though
theyre just trying to feed their kids by doing all the stupid shit no white
    person will
when was the last time you saw a white person scrubbing toilets in public
its like some white people wont be happy until were extinct

speaking of extinction
bees and rhinos and alligators
the animals are dying

the animals are disappearing
whole swaths of species
just gone
just gone

what else are we going to lose over the next ten years
thats if we even make it ten years
the way things are going the next war might be the last

and even if we were to last just a little bit longer
i mean the planets kind of over us
by the year 2050 our coasts
miami new york new orleans
philadelphia virginia beach
sacramento jacksonville
gone
they'll disappear intov the ocean

i mean
is no one terrified
does no one think of these things

sure some of you are thinking
climate change
thats not real
pretty soon were going to run out of names for all these hurricanes
and sometimes i wake up and i cant breathe
                                        a breath
so i
so i

my parents were immigrants
so i want to make a difference i said to my mom
i want our name to mean something

i was never naïve enough to say i wanted to save the world
but i did want to change it
even if
it was just a small thing

there was too much to do i told my mom
there were more important things that i had to
i was busy doing something
thats what i told my mom

i had no time for love
i had no time for some guy to to to
to

i had more important things to do
my life would not be small
my life would not be insignificant

just look at the world
just look at our home

i would focus on the things that mattered
this world that we live in
thats what matters isnt it
isnt it

thats what i told her

she believed me

                              a breath
at least i hope she did

                    cris *looks at the audience*
                                        at the **ensemble**
                              he is pleading
i am exhausted

                    and then **cris** *gets into bed*
              time stretches

the hangover.

> *a beautiful hotel room*
> > *these bitches are classy*
> > *money has been spent*
> > *the penthouse*

> **cris** *is in bed sleeping*
> *its dark because the curtains are drawn*

> > *after a moment* **eleanor** *comes in from outside*
> *(down the hall from another room*
> > *or from the living room in their suite)*
> *she stumbles around*
> > *ow!*

> > > *she cant see shit*
> *finally she OPENS the curtains as*
> > > *lights*

> > > > *pour*

> > *in*

> > > *she*

> > > > *is*

> > *fucking beautiful*

eleanor
rise and shine sleepyhead

> > *nothing*

this town is so weird
i mean not weird
its just not like
well you know what i mean

i cant believe you made us come here
i mean not made thats not the right word
i mean i would go anywhere for you
you know that
obviously
im just so surprised
this is where you

i know you decided to come back
to where it all began
which is i will admit pretty romantic
but this place
its just so unlike you

this place is
so
im trying to think of the right word and im not sure
small

that doesnt seem right

i mean that bar we went to last night
the one bar open in town
it was so
and the people
could you imagine if you lived here and that was your only
option
yes option
if thats all you knew and all you ever had to choose from
i guess you wouldnt know any better if you were from here
if youd never left
if youd never had any other exposure
but wow
i cant believe

well at least everything is cheap
i spent about a third of what we usually do

still
i never would have thought this
youre so metropolitan
                              she sits
but im grateful you made us come here
to see something else
to experience something different

we can go our whole lives and miss things that are right in front of us
we can go our whole lives and not know what is in our own backyard

its so strange to be from a place and to be completely not from it
do you know what i mean

im making no sense
i drank too much last night
we always drink too much

ill be happy to go home when this is all over though
ill say that much
i mean im happy to be here

with you
of course
like i said
ill always have had this experience

we dont all live the same do we

cris

oh come on
i know you cant possibly be sleeping
i remember when i
my nerves
i was so anxious
so happy
but so anxious

cris
honey
sweetheart get up
                        she jumps into bed with him
its your wedding day
        she gets under the blanket with him finally seeing his face
whats wrong

                        he doesnt say anything
are you okay
you can tell me anything
you know you can
im here
cris
i love you the most
you know that
what is it

cris
i cant talk to you about this

eleanor
what do you mean

cris
you wont understand

eleanor
are you having second thoughts
cold feet

cris
its not that

eleanor
we can make this whole thing stop
if thats what you want
we can get you out of here
you dont have to see anyone
me and the others
we can take care of it
its not too late

cris
it would be that easy for you
its not for me

eleanor
what does that mean

cris
i just keep thinking back to my old relationships
if you can call them that
failed experiments
failed attempts at connection

eleanor
weve all made poor choices

cris
thats just it
choice

eleanor
you can choose to marry him
or you can choose not to

cris
what if hes the only one who'll marry me

eleanor
youre crazy

cris
thats easy for you to say
youre

eleanor
what

cris
ryan and i used to have sex all the time
and we were such close friends
but it turned out he was just horny
he would never actually date me
i used to think that sexual attraction meant interest
that you would want the person
thats not true it turns out
he didnt

eleanor
which ones he

cris
kyle was married
and then he wasn't
but he still picked someone else

eleanor
fuck that guy

cris
adam was in love with me

eleanor
but he was too young

cris
was he

eleanor
thats what you said

cris
leo wanted me
and then i wanted him
and then he didnt
and so i spent years getting over it
and then he came back around and decided he couldn't live without me
even though he'd married someone else
so i opened myself back up to him

eleanor
cris

cris
and slept with him
and then he vanished

eleanor
we all need a one-night stand or two

cris
how many have you had

eleanor
me
oh
two just two

cris
ive had more one-night stands than actual relationships

eleanor
well
that doesnt mean anything
youre gay the rules are different
i can say that right

cris
doesnt it
maybe im just a stereotype
maybe im just exactly what people think i am

eleanor
dont say that
youre the most special person i know

cris
how many times have you broken up with someone

eleanor
what
i dont understand the question
like how many relationships have i had

cris
no
how many people
have you dumped

eleanor
i dont understand what you mean

cris
okay fine
since we have known each other
how many relationships have you been in

eleanor
cris

cris
are you helping or not

eleanor
well i mean im married now but before
she starts counting on her fingers
her lips moving along with her
john
anchorage
three
nyu
twitter
six
there have been six

cris
and how many of those guys have broken up with you

eleanor
youre being crazy

cris
i bet none of them have
not one

eleanor
whats your point

cris
youll never fundamentally understand me

eleanor
i love you more than anyone

cris
you keep saying that

eleanor
its true

cris
i know it is
but it doesnt change the fundamental truths about who we are
the gulf between us
you can know
but you cant feel
not really

eleanor
i love you
i love you

cris
everyone loves me
but no one wants to be with me
im no ones first choice
to be wanted more than anything
at the expense of
everything else
ill never know that

eleanor
this guy does
dave does

cris
am i settling

eleanor
do you love him

a moment

cris
yes

eleanor
then

cris
you dont see
you dont see
not the way i do

eleanor
then well find someone else

cris
i envy you
i envy you and i resent you

she is stunned

eleanor
cris

cris
and the sad thing is
you havent done anything wrong
its not your fault
you dont deserve this
but its the truth
youre you and im me
and nothing will ever change that

theres a knock on the door

eleanor
not now

the knocking gets intense
it gets loud

eleanor
were not
cris
you have to listen to me

cris *goes to open the door*

eleanor *is crushed*
she sits down somewhere
by the window
at the corner of the bed
her bright bright eyes are drained

as **cris** *opens the door*
diego *burts in*
hes wasted

niegel *is right next to him*
trying to calm him down

a frozen tableau

eleanor *turns to the audience*
all the color drained from the world

eleanor
its hard to realize
you hurt the one you love most in the world
simply by existing
                    the tableau breaks and **diego** *and* **niegel** *burst in*

diego
where is he
you

cris
who

niegel
im so sorry

diego
we have to talk
RIGHT NOW

cris
diego this isnt a good time

diego
you are going to sit down and you are going to listen to me before you
    ruin your life

cris
what the fuck
are you drunk

diego
fuck you im not drunk

cris
youre wasted
niegel

niegel
i tried to get him to stop
to get him to sleep

cris
sleep

diego
im not a child
youre not my babysitter

cris
you havent slept
since last night

diego
you have to call the wedding off

cris
what no
what is he
diego
what did you guys—

niegel
me
ive been trying to keep him in check

cris
ive never seen him this way
he doesnt actually like to drink
you dont ever drink
how did you
why did you
diego

diego
i just need to talk

cris
so talk

diego
you cant trust him

cris
are you high
are you sniffling
coke
did you do
what is going on

niegel
come on diego
just a quick shower and a nap
well get you good and ready

cris
my weddings in a few hours
how could you do this to me

diego
do this to you
im trying to help you
im trying to be the good brother
unlike you
all selfish
and me me me me me
ALWAYS ME ME ME ME

                              niegel *tries to drag* **diego** *off*

niegel
come on

diego
get off me

    diego *spins around drunkenly flailing*
            he tries to punch **niegel** *but he misses and trips over himself*
   he goes
                    CRASHING
       to the
           floor
                        and then the door opens
                        its **dave**

he looks amazingly handsome
          already in his tuxedo

dave
whats going on
i heard yelling down the hall

cris
youre not supposed to be here
youre not supposed to see me before

diego
see you
HA
youre a man
or did you forget

eleanor
thats enough diego

dave
im sorry i know you care
about tradition or whatever
but i was worried
i heard
i thought something might have happened to you
i ran over as quickly as i could
im sorry if

cris
you shouldn't have

dave
my instincts are to protect you
to make sure youre okay
to run towards danger not away from

diego
oh shut the fuck up

> **cris** *kneels to the ground*
> *he puts his arms around* **diego**

cris
hey
will you stop it
its my wedding day
listen to me
everything's okay
were all here
im here
just relax
okay
calm down

diego
i am calm

cris
good

diego
tell him

cris
what

diego
tell him

niegel
tell him what

diego
not you
YOU
tell him

dave
i dont know what hes talking about

diego
if you dont fucking tell him
i swear to god
ill kick your ass
sin verguenza
come mierda

cris
diego

diego
PINCHE MARICON
ERES UN MARICON
tell him
or have you no balls

dave
seriously bro
what the fuck

diego
fine then
i will
last night after i left you
after i
i went for a walk
and i wanted another
we were celebrating so
so i went to this place
they were open late and i saw him there

cris
him

diego
your fiancé
at first i couldn't tell it was him
his face was turned in the other direction
but i recognized his posture

dave
diego

diego
and there was this young
this little blond thing
this tiny guero
this guerrito with
first he was kissing his neck
just licking it
his tongue all out and shit
and then he was kissing his chest
and i

and i
i just stood there
because i
i dont know why
i was too—

dave
you were drunk

diego
fuck you
i know what i saw

cris
diego

diego
im not done yet
im not
                    a breath
he
he was kissing on him
and then i see that his hand

it was in his
in his
and theyre making out so i still cant see his face
but then the little guerrito hand
and then i see his face pulls back
his mouth open
barely able to breathe and its
its

diego *just slouches back unable to say anything else*

everyone is frozen in silence

eventually **cris** *gets up*

cris
niegel will you help him to the shower
a cold bath and a quick nap will help him
help him

eleanor
cris

diego
did you hear what i said

hes cheating on you
on the night before your wedding
hes cheating on you
i saw it with my own eyes
i promise

cris
i know

eleanor
what

dave
we have

cris
dont you fucking say anything right now

diego
what do you mean you know

cris
we have an understanding

rules
hes
were allowed

diego
youre just a bitch

cris
please
not now

diego
when you came out
do you remember what papi said
our papi who loved you and took care of you
our papi who never turned his back on you

cris
please dont

diego
papi said its okay that youre gay
its okay
just promise me you wont be one of those maricones who wears a dress

cris
im not i said
i never wanted to be that type of gay

eleanor
and so what if you were

diego
but this is worse

cris
please dont say that

diego
youre marrying a guy who uses you
for what
our parents money paid for this
now i know why
because youre the girl right
this is youre dowry
youre the bitch
were paying him to take you off our hands

youre the bitch in the relationship
youre taking it like a bitch
maricon
you might as well be wearing a dress

                diego *slowly gets up to leave*

diego
thank god our parents werent here to see this
for the first time in my life
im grateful theyre dead

                he goes

niegel
ill—

cris
no
let him go
youve done enough
hes not your responsibility

        a breath

           a big breath
      no one knows what to do
        too afraid that the ice is about to crack beneath them
    and then
will you just
just get to the
i think the guests will be arriving soon

niegel
whatever you need

           niegel *leaves*

                eleanor *and* **dave** *remain*
    frozen

eleanor
what diego said
its not—

cris
no
hes right
hes one hundred percent right

dave
we had an—

cris
i told you i didnt want to know about it
whatever you did
it was fine
as long as you kept it to yourself

dave
it was my last night and i was drunk

cris
youve humiliated me

dave
cris im—

cris
dont come near me
dont touch me
dont

dave
babe

a breath

       a moment

cris
i used to love when you called me that
that word
and the sound of your voice
now itll just be a reminder
now itll just be one more thing i hate about you
eleanor
will you help me get ready
its almost time

      he goes

          eleanor *gives dave one long*
              deep
                  painful look

cris
eleanor

she goes

dave *stands there*
alone

dave
this isnt the version of the story
our story
i wish youd seen

this isnt the version of me—
                    he pauses
its not always about me
i know that
but

i want to tell you about what it is like to love cris
loving cris has been the great
gift
opportunity
accomplishment
i dont know
i dont know what the right word is
all i know is that of all the things in my life
being the one to love cris has been the thing i am most proud of
he chose me
i chose him
we chose each other
that is so rare
these days

but

that doesnt mean its been easy

its hard to love someone who barely loves themselves
to cris i was unattainable
i was perfection

but when i fell in love with him
i dont know
in a way
to him
it meant that something was wrong with me
because how could anyone sane ever love him
its a catch twenty-two
do you see

its exhausting always trying to convince someone of your feelings for
   them

i didnt want an open relationship because i needed to sleep with other
   people
i wanted an open relationship because i thought
he would be the one i would always go back to
he would be the one i would always choose
he would be the thing i couldn't live without
i wanted to show him that
i thought he would see
instead

i feel stuck
i feel like im in a corner
i feel like i cant win

i cant control the narrative
according to him im this perfect thing

but
if you could see whats in my head
it would terrify you

narrative

these are the moments of our life together that you have seen
they were picked for you

but its not what i want to leave you with

i want to tell you about the things that are beautiful

i want to tell you about the time i introduced cris to my father
and how when my father hugged him

i felt like this wound that had been bleeding for years
finally scabbed over

i want to tell you about how for fifteen years
we had a dog named tennessee
named after the playwright
not the state
who slept between us and saw the world with us
a perfect family

i want to tell you about the time i said i love you to him for the first time
and how i finally knew what those words meant

that until you know
you dont

i want to tell you a story about two people who met and fell in love
and built their own universe

because its real
and it happened
and you should know
its possible

thats the story i want to leave you with

he starts to go

oh
and our production of our town
i wish i could tell you it was a big hit
but after what happened with pearl and emily
the whole thing was called off
it was pretty terrible to be honest
and thats the story i could tell you

but instead ill say
the play was a disaster but we found each other
and thats what's most important to me

and then

sarah *and* **pearl** *come out*

sarah
you should—

dave
yea

and he goes off

sarah
i knew we shouldn't have
i told you
we should have stuck to the script
i dont know why we let cris—

pearl
its too late now

sarah
order

i just like order
theres a proper way and theres

pearl
what
your way

sarah
thats not

pearl
yes it is

sarah
anyway
its done now
i just dont like showing ugly things

pearl
but things arent always pretty
things arent always easy or correct or

sarah
my father used to have a saying

pearl
oh yeah
i cant wait to hear it

sarah
never air out your dirty laundry in public

pearl
sarah
everyones father had that saying

sarah
well

pearl
youre actually not as unique as you think you are

sarah
thats—

pearl
as you have all already surmised its a wedding day

sarah
weddings are supposed to be happy

WEDDING DAY

pearl
also
in case you were wondering
i am dead
or i mean
the character you saw me playing in the last act
in the car
she died

sarah
but thats not what today is about

pearl
no
i guess it isnt

sarah
so were going to get ready but we want to leave you with a friend

pearl
some of you might have actually paid for her services before

sarah
thats a weird way—

pearl
shut up sarah
the wedding planner

sarah
the wedding planner

no one comes out

pearl
the WEDDING planner

still nothing

sarah
HELLO

*the **wedding planner** rushes out*

wedding planner
i am so sorry
after that move you guys pulled

sarah
i was against it

wedding planner
i had some damage to undo

pearl
im afraid to ask

wedding planner
nothing to worry about
i am good at my job
i am the best at my job
i took care of it
the wedding will go on
or as you theater people say
the show must go on

                    a sigh of relief from **pearl** *and* **sarah**

pearl
well

sarah
well leave you to it

wedding planner
people always ask me why i decided to be a wedding planner
i find that most people these days are so negative
they throw facts at me
more than fifty percent of couples get divorced
they say things
if the gays were smart they would leave marriage alone
why take on all the trouble

but i love weddings
the way people come together

i didnt have siblings growing up
and yes my parents were divorced
they divorced before i was six so i dont even remember them ever being
    together
ive only ever known them as individuals
anyway my parents lived on opposite coasts so
making friends
building relationships was complicated
back then we didnt have all the gadgets

the facetime
and the facebook
all the face things
so it was hard to really build relationships
summers i spent alone wandering around
the school year i was in school and no one really cared about me
i mean
i think because i didnt see them over the summer
they sort of forgot about me
forgot i existed
so it was hard to build any real relationships

sorry
i dont know why im telling you this
what this has to do

i love weddings

have you ever noticed that weddings are like small universes
you and you will get together and youll create a new universe
or you and you and thatll be a different universe
or you and you and
well now we have a galaxy

on a wedding day people will come together and some youll know
a cousin you havent seen in five years
a friends friend you met once in high school
but then theres also the people you have no connection to
except these two people who have brought you all together

and for this one day
this one weekend
you have created a small universe
with all these people
all these different types of people from different places
with different lives and stories and histories
and they all come together for you
and create something new
something beautiful
this is yours

this is your own personal world

i know sometimes people get divorced
i know sometimes things end
but for me

why jump ahead
for me
this is how ill remember you
this is my beginning middle and end

i get to see the beautiful thing you created
and then i go home
and thats what i take with me

> *the* **ensemble** *comes out*
> *they are the* **guests** *and they are also* **ensemble**

1
cris and i went to high school together
he was my prom date

2
im cris' mother's best friend's daughter
she would have loved this
cris and i dont really know each other that well
im honored to be here

3
im daves best friend

4
im daves best friend

5
im daves ex-boyfriend

6
it took me three planes and a bus to get here
im speaking a foreign language to you right now but the magic of theater
    is making it possible for you
to understand me

7
two people at this wedding will meet tonight for the first time
they will have the best sex either of them has ever had
the woman will get pregnant but she wont tell the man
she'll die of stomach cancer without ever telling her daughter who her
    father really is

8
i spent two thousand dollars on this wedding
the flights

the room
the gifts
the truth is i couldn't afford it
i cant afford it
but what are you supposed to do you know
because of my choice
ill fall back on my rent
ill have late fees
ill eventually get kicked out
i wont know it all started here

9
i am a tv star
you dont know my name but youve seen me on all your favorite tv
    shows

10
i am a movie star
you know exactly who i am

11
every time i come to a wedding i think
i wonder if ill hook up with anyone tonight
that may make me seem slutty
but the truth is
im just desperate for someone to hold me

12
ive never been to a gay wedding before
i think theyre strange
who pays for what

13
the gays have the best weddings
trust me
weve been missing out

14
cris and i used to be friends
im surprised he invited me
if im being honest
i used to be
i am
i have always been in love with cris
but i could never tell him

so instead
i pushed him away

i ruined our friendship
i think he invited me because he feels he has to
for old times sake
i came here thinking i might finally tell him the truth
and i dont kow
maybe stop the wedding
is that terrible
i think hes in love with me too
if only i could be honest

1
what do you do

2
how do you know cris

3
are you with dave or cris

4
what side are you sitting on

5
bride or groom

6
you mean groom or groom

7
do i

8
where are you from

9
did you travel far

10
im nearby

11
who's side are you on

12
what do you do

13
i havent seen you for a while

howve you been

niegel
i spent a lot of time thinking about what to do with my life
at first i wanted to make an impact
and then i just wanted to make my parents proud
i saw so many of my friends becoming lawyers
cops
doing government jobs
some went corporate some went nonprofit
all of them were satisfied
none of them were happy
and thats a sad thing you know
you have one life to live
ideally anyway
why not make the best of what you have
the super-idealistic ones
they were the least happy
they watched as time went by
faster and faster
and things stayed the same

did you know this thing about time
that the longer you live
the faster time passes to you
okay let me try to explain it
when a baby is born
they have no concept of time
and then one day were like happy birthday
this is the one year mark
so then when their second year is passing
a year seems like forever because thats all they have known
thats all they have lived
and so
in this way
time is relative
when you turn ten and your parents say you cant do this until your
    twenty
that seems like so far from now
like forever
because you have to wait as long as you have already lived

in other words
you have to wait your whole life
but when youre fifty or sixty
one year goes by so fast
it flies
it speeds past you
because the longer youve lived
the more you have to compare it to

when youre seventy and someone says you only have ten years left to live
man
that time goes
in a blink of an eye

so i think about that
i think about time
i think about being happy
i think about making a difference

so i decided to be an anthropologist
i bet you dont know any anthropolgists
most people dont know what anthropoligists even do

okay
so an anthropologist
studies
the origins
social customs
and beliefs of humankind

so basically
we study humans

heres an assignment i give my students

lets say a tootbrush
if you had to pick up a toothbrush and explain what it does
or why we need it
to an alien
how would you do so

for starters
its a piece of plastic
about five inches long
some are different colors
but that doesnt matter

there are bristles on the end
they are rough enough to withstand scrubbing
which is this action
but they are not so rough that they may hurt you
this is important because you put them into the sensitive area known as
    your mouth
and your gums are sensitive

basically
when the planet ends
and an alien comes down here

and starts digging around amongst the dirt and garbage and history and
    trash
when he finds that toothbrush
will he or she know what its for

what about a gun

the choices our government makes
the actions they leave behind
their legacy
its not just words in a history book
but instead
a very real thing that will affect our future
our present
our—

i wonder about what we leave behind
i wonder about what we leave behind and how well explain it to other
    people
i wonder how well explain it to aliens from distant universes
i wonder how well explain it to our children

i think what we leave behind
i think it matters

cris *enters*

cris
hey
sorry

niegel
no worries
this is your day

cris
i wanted to apologize for earlier

niegel
you have nothing to apologize for

cris
well
regardless
i wanted to apologize and i wanted to thank you
for dealing with it

niegel
youre family
were all family now

we take the bad with the good dont we
                              cris *smiles*

cris
do you know where diego is
the wedding planner
shes freaking out
hes not answering his phone and were already late

niegel
ill go look for him

cris
thanks
really

niegel
of course
and hey
im not into dudes
but if i was
youd be it
you look amazing today

cris
youre a mess
get out of here

niegel *leaves*

cris pauses for a moment
he takes everyone in
he takes everything in

and maybe
for a moment
all we see
the entire space
it becomes the universe
and we are all a part of it

cris is an ancient explorer discovering the galaxy

cris
i got used to being alone

dave
im here now

cris
things changed because of you

dave
for the better

cris
i was less cold

dave
we learned a new language together

cris
we discovered something only we knew about

dave
i stopped worrying so much

cris
i started worrying more

dave
oh

cris
afraid wed drift apart

dave
impossible

cris
you say that now

dave
i have a secret

cris
we all have secrets

dave
i always thought you were too good for me

cris
but then you got to know me

dave
theres all this space

look at all this space

cris
youre deflecting

dave
look at this vast endlessness
so much we dont know
so much we havent discovered
so much we dont know yet

cris
too much

dave
not enough

cris
look
a shooting star

a star shoots across the universe
dave *goes after it*

cris
youre like a puppy
everything distracts you

dave
its so beautiful

it gets darker

cris
where did you go

nothing

dave

nothing

come back

nothing

dave
i cant see you
i cant hear you

nothing

where did you go

nothing

dave i dont know where you are
i dont know where i am
weve gone too far

nothing

ive got to turn back
dave
dave
dave
which way is back
which way is home

and then we are back at the wedding
real life

eleanor
did you hear me

cris
what

eleanor
shes here

cris
who

pearl
that girl

cris
what girl

                                        dave *walks in*

dave
cant you
you guys please
shes just standing in the back
no one has to know shes here

pearl
we know

cris
what girl

eleanor
emily

cris
dave

dave
look
i dont understand why you hate her so much
why you care

pearl
are you fucking kidding me
that girl is a monster
that girl is a murderer

cris
she didnt actually kill anyone

dave
thank you

pearl
i thought you were on my side

cris
i am i mean

eleanor
i thought the whole thing made you sick

cris
it does
i agree
she shouldn't be here

dave
if she was this monster you all make her out to be shes be in prison
wouldnt she

eleanor
thats your excuse

pearl
lets be clear about one thing
the only reason shes not in prison for telling that girl to kill herself
that girl that is now dead and buried thanks to that psycho
is because the girl who is dead was black
lets all be clear about that

dave
dont you ever get tired of playing the race card

pearl
im leaving

cris
no stay
please

dave
she made a mistake
havent you ever made a mistake before

cris
yea i guess i have

dave
cris

cris
she leaves
its her or me

dave
shes my sister

cris
i know that you werent raised like us
so at best youre incredibly stupid
at worst youre just a terribly myopic
selfish white guy

dave
this is why youre going to end up alone
because youre afraid
so you find whatever reason you can to push people away
and thats
its just sad
youre not going to do any better than me

cris
throw a tantrum
its the end for people like you

a commotion is heard offstage
                    its frantic
        everyone turns to look at where the noise is coming from

              and then **niegel** *appears*
he is in his black and white tuxedo
                    except its no longer black and white
        its covered in blood

niegel
im sorry
i tried but i couldn't stop
i couldn't handle

eleanor
whats going on

pearl
what happened

niegel
im sorry

dave
what

niegel
its diego

cris
diego

niegel
i thought he stopped drinking
i thought he got in the shower and slept it off
but he didnt
he kept drinking and found more coke
he was wandering the streets
drunk
just wasted
a total mess
yelling
and the cops
they tried to
they tried to
but he wouldnt
and he got
he was out of control
i tried to get him to stop
to calm down

but he wouldnt
and then he
he grabbed
and they
and they
im sorry
hes gone
hes—

                        niegel *slides down to the floor*

cris
i wish i never came here
i wish wed never met
i wish—

                                        cris *slides down to the floor*
                        dave *tries to hug him*
        cris *is silent*

cris
you werent worth this
no one is

and then in a moment of theatrical magic
diego *appears*
he is in spotlight
the whole world looking at him
he talks to the audience

diego
wow
so this is what this feels like

i know im supposed to come out here and tell you that
that if i hadn't been killed today
i would have gone on to greatness
that i would have accomplished something huge
something important
that i would have led a revolution
or discovered a new world
or a cure for
that i would have saved lives
that my life
that my life
my life would have been extraordinary

and maybe that would make a difference to you
it probably would

but the truth is

im just
i was
just an ordinary man
who would have led an ordinary life
i never wanted more than that
i never wanted the weight of the world on my shoulders
that overbearing
exhausting weight

people kept telling me that i had to be different
that i had to be more
to prove to others that we could not only be as good as them
but better
to prove that we werent just average or basic
to prove that our lives mean something

mean something

but why should that be my responsibility
all i wanted was to be ordinary
that was enough for me

so i guess knowing that makes it better doesnt it
makes it okay
now that they've killed me
now that im dead

they didnt kill anybody special
its not that big of a loss

im just one less ordinary man

and then

. . . we transform into act three.

the final act: *"death"*

transformation.

        diego *stands in front of us*
           and then
                behind him
the space
    T

      R
      A   *N*   *S*
             FORMS
and this is what we are looking at
        imagine this space
      imagine that you are looking directly at a square box
     just a square
       picture it

         now in that square
          from the bottom to the top
  the square is filled with dirt

       dirt
          dirt
             dirt
dirt
      dirt
      dirt
      dirt
      dirt

         three-fourths of the box is dirt
   now when we get to the top
      when three-fourths of the box are dirt
    we see some grass
      grass is the top layer
        and maybe a tree
         and some roots
     if there were people standing on this grass
you would only see from their feet to maybe the bottom of their knees

now

one more thing

in the dirt

youll notice that there are tons of bodies

bodies everywhere

the bodies have been buried there

six feet under

but also ten feet under

and four feet under

they are everywhere

some are more fresh

but most of them are in different states of decay

we see our entire **ensemble** there

we see **cris** at the center

we also see **dave**

are they buried next to each   other??

as the space transforms

diego watches us

and then he turns and

takes his place amongst the dead

times passes

and in that time

the sound of heartbreak

the sound of a baby being born

the sound of an old woman dying

the sound of an engine

an old transistor radio

the sound of a bomb going off

an explosion

the sound of cheering

the sound of sobbing

the sound of clocks ticking

many clocks

the sound of death

the sound of life

the sound of birth

the sound of heartbreak

the sound of heartbreak

the sound of heartbreak

the sound of heartbreak

the sound of life passing us by

the sound of another explosion

and then a flash of light

rain

rain

rain

the sun

another flash of light

chirping

chirping

chirping

and another explosion

and then

fog and the sound of dusk

a young man approaches

well call him **gatz**

he is pacing

he sits

he stands

he paces

he paces

he leans against a tree

time passes

and then a young woman enters

she is breathless

well call her **red**

gatz
i was so worried

red
i told you id be here didnt i

gatz
you did

red
i promised

gatz
i was so scared

red
i never break a promise

gatz
are you alone

red
no one knows im here

gatz
you were careful

red
i always am

gatz
i thought i was never going to see you again

> *they embrace*
> *its tight*
> *they dont let go for a while*

gatz
let me look at you

red
ive aged

gatz
we all have

red
your family

gatz
lost

red
when

gatz
a while back
before the second storm

red
im here now

gatz
youre like a dream

red
did you have trouble finding

gatz
your directions were good

red
you burned them after

gatz
of course

red
no one can know

gatz
no one knows im here

red
good

gatz
what is this place

red
an old burial ground
when they ran out of space
they just

gatz
no names anywere

red
there wasn't time
theres a rumor my mom and dad were buried here
and my grandparents too
somewhere underneath all this
dirt

gatz
your lineage

red
my history
where i came from

gatz
where it all began

> **gatz** *bends down and kisses the ground*
> **red** *smiles*
>> *they sit together*
>> *and hold hands*

gatz
the captain says he thinks the war will be over soon

red
they always say that
they've been saying that for years
as far back as we can remember

gatz
what does blue think

red
dead

gatz
what

red
they got him after the third rebellion

gatz
im sorry

red
its the world we live in i guess

gatz
he was brave

red
he had to be
we all do

gatz
lets run away

red
where

gatz
somewhere that isnt like this

red
dont be silly

gatz
there must be some untouched place
we can be explorers
find an untouched part of this world that isnt

red
what

gatz
ruined

red
start all over

gatz
just the two of us

red
youre such a dreamer
what is that

gatz
an old transistor radio
over forty years old

red
does it work

gatz
of course

red
you were always amazing with wires
my engineer
play something

julio iglesisas song plays

gatz
i dont know how much longer i can do this

red
you have to be strong

gatz
youre leaving again arent you

red
i have to

gatz
if you go ill kill myself

red
dont say that

gatz
theres no point in

red
i love you

gatz
so what

red
dont be like that

gatz
whats the point

red
i just have one more thing to do
one more mission
and then i promise
we can go wherever you want

gatz
let me come with you

red
you know i cant do that

gatz
but were on the same side

red
they wont understand
they'll hurt you

gatz
please

red
ill come back

gatz
no you wont

red
ive never broken a promise have i

gatz
whatever

red
have i

gatz
no

gatz *paces*

gatz
i thought the end of the world would be more beautiful
i thought the apocalypse would be like a thunderstorm
instead
its just one
long
im exhausted

red
i have to do this **gatz**
theres a possibility
if i do this
the war might end
and then
we can be
we can be
do you understand

gatz
why cant someone else

red
if not me then who

gatz
anyone
anyone else
i dont care

red
and if they dont

gatz
its not my problem

red
you cant think like that
if we do were no better than they are
listen to me
i dont want to hide
i dont want to run away
a life like that
its not worth living
but if i do this
theres a possibility of something better
of a world worth being a part of
do you hear me

gatz
at what cost

red
gatz—

gatz
no
dont you understand
these things come with a price
if i lose you
what point is there in living in a world
no matter how good
if you arent in it

red
sometimes we have to sacrifice—

gatz
no no no
its always us who have to do the sacrificing
its always us who have to turn the other cheek
its always us who have to rise
well im done
im done
i will not keep giving up parts of who i am
for what

red
i love you okay

this silences **gatz**
a long
quiet
painful moment

red
say it back

gatz
no

red
come on
say it back

gatz
youll leave me

red
this will be the last time
i promise

gatz
. . . . . .

red
come on
i have to go

gatz
no

red
please

gatz
i wont
i dont

red
im doing this for you
im doing this for us

gatz
please

red
i have to go

i love you

gatz
no

red
im leaving
i love you

gatz
no

red
i love you
i love you
i love you

                              red *starts to go*

gatz
wait

                        red *turns*

gatz
i love you

red
soon this will all be over

                            red *goes*
                                      gatz *sits*
                  he cries
                        he cries
                              he falls asleep
                  and then we hear other footseps
                                    we see boots
                  the boots pause
                              they see **gatz**
                  we hear the sound of a pistol being cocked
                                          a gunshot
            gatz *slumps over*

                  THIS IS HOW IT ENDS.

a cautionary tail

by christopher oscar peña

this ones for

andrea lauer
*who has brought her beautiful design and even
more beautiful friendship to all these plays*

a cautionary tail was originally commissioned by NYU's Graduate Acting Program (Mark Wing-Davey, Artistic Director).

It had its world premiere at the Flea Theatre (Jim Simpson, Artistic Director) in New York City. Opening night was June 10, 2013.

It was directed by Benjamin Kamine.

SCENIC DESIGN	David Meyer
LIGHTING DESIGN	Jonathan Cottle
COSTUME DESIGN	Andrea Lauer
SOUND DESIGN	Jeremy S. Bloom
MOVEMENT DIRECTOR	Laura Brandel
PRODUCTION STAGE MANAGER	Anne Huston

The cast was as follows:

TIGER/TIN	Bobby Foley
VIVIENNE	Cleo Gray
LUKE	Tony Vo
DEREK	Barron Bass
KAELAN	Stephen Stout
BRANDI	Madeleine Bundy
KOREN	Bonnie Milligan
JOANNA	Marlowe Holden
SONYA	Jacquelyn Revere
TRAVELING SALESMAN/ JACK/WILLIAM	Alex Grubbs
ENSEMBLE	Alton Alburo, Matt Bovee, Jenelle Chu, Sasha Diamond, Karen Eilbacher, Aaron Parker Fouhey, Alex J. Gould, Christine Lee, and Evan Maltby
The following actors joined the ENSEMBLE at extension:	Krystina Bailey, Orlando Rivera, Kate Thulin, and Ramon Olmos Torres

a cautionary tail had a workshop production at the Atlas Theatre at NYU Grad Acting, December 1–5, 2012.

It was directed by Kyle Fabel.

SCENIC DESIGN	Rebecca Philips
LIGHTING DESIGN	Anshuman Bhatia

COSTUME DESIGN	Kathleen Doyle
SOUND DESIGN	Fitz Patton
MOVEMENT DIRECTOR	Whitney Hunter
PRODUCTION STAGE MANAGER	Anne Huston

The cast was as follows:

TIGER/TIN	David Lam
VIVIENNE	Ruibo Qian
LUKE	Julian Cihi
DEREK	Robbie Williams
KAELAN	Ross Cowan
BRANDI/JOANNA	Anne Troup
KOREN/SONYA	Marinda Anderson
TRAVELING SALESMAN/	
JACK/WILLIAM	Andrew Hovelson
DANCER/ENSEMBLE	Dina Shihabi

characters

luke wood—seventeen. impulsive. a very american, chinese boy

vivienne wood—eighteen. calm. thoughtful. strong willed. trying to make it work

the tiger—an androgynous leader. the mother(fucker) who rules this jungle
also plays **tin wong** an asian man who has lost his way

derek—vivienne's boyfriend. eighteen. a black man who is japanese

brandi—a rich, bitchy, white girl. thinks shes so cool. lukes bff
also plays **joanna davidowitz** thirties. corporate power chick

koren—another one of lukes bffs. wiser than brandi. loves to sing. lesbian?
also plays **sonya washington** thirties. wears the pants. power woman at the office

kaelan burke—super-hot. hipster musician type. grounded. open and exploring

old-fashioned traveling salesman—just that. and magical. loves his job. secretly nice
also plays **william grant** coporate guy. snarky. enjoys his job, which is like fucked-up
also plays **jack** an unkempt, but charming man. the guy who means it

setting

new york city
       the wood family apartment—
             the living room
             viviennes room
             lukes room
       a record store: OTHER MUSIC
       a park in chinatown
       a corporate office
       across the street from a kids private school (say st. annes)
       an office in china
the jungle: the tigers den

time

a few years ago and a few years from now

        and a place right in the middle that stretches on forever

notes

—it is important that the jungle world feel different from the rest of the play

—this play works best when it moves quickly, expertly, fluidly, and things bleed into each other

—this play is about opposites. east meets west. tradition versus progress. speed and stagnancy. old and new. the past and the future. holding on and forgetting. the more you play with theatricalizing these themes, the better.

—the gestures are meant to act as a physical representation of forward movement, progression that is too fast, a ground that we cant stand on, because we are searching for balance. its meant to contrast the normal paced-ness of everything else that is happening. sometimes we, our minds, the world, are moving faster than we think – let the actors experience this and make it real in the moments where it is listed.

—this play loves sound and light and dark and shadows and fragments and missing pieces.

—i imagine the dance breaks being hipster/ambience rock: girls, my gold mask, deerhunter, twin shadow, neon indian, washed-out, the 1975, muse, etc. etc.

—finally, the first act of this play should feel like a neon pop music video. it should feel like the movie spring breakers. and the second act should feel like kids, all the color drained away. think of it as a homage.

act one.

scene.

                darkness
                    the kind of darkness you might find in a cave
         sounds of dripping
                water
            sounds of
       whipping
            air
            sounds of deep breathing in a cave
       almost as if the cave is alive
            and then light punctuates the air
                     fighting its way in
                  the entire **cast**
             save **the tiger**
               comes out

1
a myth

2
a story

3
a truth

4
a place to begin

5
where to begin

6
at the very beginning

7
too late for that

8
somewhere in the middle

9
somewhere where the past has already affected the present

10
a place with baggage

11
heavy baggage

12
history

13
a myth

14
a story

15
a truth

16
a true story

17
a made-up story

18
a place from which to move forward

19
a place not to go

20
before its too late

21
its already too late

22
or is it

23
a tiger

all
a tiger

> **the tiger** *reveals itself*
>   *first in darkness*
> *a silhouette*
>   *and then it emerges*

regal and proud
         the tiger *is fabulous and fabulously dressed*
high-fashion couture
         she is an androgynous beast of beauty
she speaks to those who it commands
                  she is posed and in control
         of
                  every
         syllable

the tiger
you must regard tradition
tradition is history
tradition is order
you must respect the natural order of the universe
of mother and father
ancient rules cast on stone never to be forgotten
keep tradition and the world keeps spinning
break with tradition and suffer the consequences
of all those who have come before
my will is your law
because i know better than you
only when you have lived
only when you have experienced
only when you have followed the paths marked out for you
only then will you understand
only then will you be wise
until then you are just a fool
and that is what i am here for
to lead you until you are not

                  with a wave of her hand, the **ensemble** *vanishes*
                  and then **the tiger**
                  breaks
                           the tiger *breaks and her*
                  well her
                  her real ATTITUDE is exposed
         she is a
         DIVA

the tiger
so here is the thing
its simple really
just do as i say

you may not understand now
but you will someday
and then you will love me
and kiss me
and thank me
and say
tiger tiger
you were right
you were right the whole time
and i will not say i told you so
because i
i am not that kind of tiger
instead i will hug you and lick your face and say
well
i told you so
im only doing it because i love you
love
what a strange word
so do as i say
and dont question me
dont push my boundaries
because if you do
i might eat you up
get in my way and i will crush you
im only doing whats best for you

                              and then with a flick of her wrist
              the **ensemble** *emerges from the shadows*
                          and then a dance
              a ritualistic calling out
                      the dance
                            the ritual
                  the movement is not realistic
                          it is stylized
                          and harsh
                          and precise
                              it is made up of gestures
              some gestures are done by everyone at the same time
          others are broken up
  and done by only a few
                          it is chaotic
                  and frenetic

and schizophrenic
some of the gestures are
a tai chi exercise
a chinese dance
the playing of a violin
over and over
and over and over and over
and over and over
another tai chi exercise
banging your head against a wall
rocking out to an eighties british rock song
playing the piano
dancing like youre madonna in front of an audience
a gesture that symbolizes a starvation for affection
starvation for love
a hug
another tai chi exercise
another chinese dance
east meets west
running fast with no energy at the end
the snapping of a photograph
writing kanji in the sky
as then the ritual is over
and everything vanishes.

scene.

      new york city
      a park in chinatown
        a park bench
      maybe a chain-link fence surrounding a basketball court
its early in the evening

     derek *sits on a park bench looking around*
       he is seventeen
       a strong-framed black man
       he seems quiet
         introspective
     he is hard to read
       he is looking for something
    or someone
       checks his watch
     do people still wear those?
       he checks his iphone

        in another part of the park
          there is a STATUE OF A MAN
      the statue is dressed in a suit
      the type an old **traveling salesman** *might wear*
      the statue is PURPLE from head to toe
    in its hand it holds his hat . . . upside down
    his briefcase is on the floor in front of him . . . open

sounds of the city
   a honk here
      a car there
   we hear a song that seems old
     from another time
       another place
   because it is
   an old chinese song
    muffled words
   it is haunting
    and then

         vivienne *arrives*
          shes also seventeen
       rushed
        shes very pretty with sad eyes

vivienne
sorry

derek
i was starting to think you werent going to show up

vivienne
i told you i was on my way

derek
thirty minutes ago

vivienne
it took me twenty minutes to convince my brother to keep his mouth shut
   and cover for me

derek
whys your brother such a little dick

vivienne
i dont know
hes just immature

derek
how much time do we have

vivienne
an hour
shes taking the 7.15 train back from connecticut

derek
i wonder if your mom will ever stop being so overbearing

vivienne
she just wants us to do well
thats all
im supposed to be practicing the violin right now

derek
do you even like playing that thing

vivienne
i dont know

a moment

vivienne
id rather be taking pictures
but she doesnt think photography is a viable career

derek
why do you do it

vivienne
to appease her

derek
i meant take pictures

vivienne
see that spot

she points at a spot in the distance

vivienne
when i was younger
there was this guy that would come out and have his lunch here every
    day at the same time
he would sit here and watch everyone
take in the sun
take in the noise
and he would talk to anyone who would listen
i was always fascinated by his stories
he was this hippie thai guy
big hair
had a son in stockholm
worked as a masseur in a little storefront around the corner thats now
    a deli
one day he told me
today i say goodbye to you
he was leaving for australia that night to see about a girl
thats what he said
to see about a girl
never saw him again after that
and now sometimes
i start to forget what he looks like

she pulls the camera up to her face and snaps a picture

vivienne
one day itll be too late you know

a moment

vivienne
are you scared

derek
of what
no

vivienne
everyone is scared of something

derek
what is there to be afraid of

vivienne
change
big decisions
wrong decisions
these moments

derek
were not the first high schoolers to have to pick which college to go to

vivienne
i got into harvard

derek
so thats it then

vivienne
i didnt say that

derek
what else is there
im going to school in california
loyola is the only place that gave me money
im not like you
i didnt get full rides to westmont
and nyu
and ucla
and penn
i have to take it

vivienne
thats not my fault

derek
whats that supposed to mean

vivienne
nothing

derek
no say it

vivienne
i didnt mean anything by it

derek
i want to hear you say it vivienne

vivienne
i told you to work harder

derek
so now im not smart enough for you right
now im not good enough

vivienne
thats not what i said
being smart and working hard are two different things

derek
so im lazy

vivienne
im not saying youre anything
stop putting words in my mouth

derek
thats what it sounds like

vivienne
i just
i wish this was easier

derek
well it isnt

vivienne
i know

silence
                    a moment
        like that moment on a windshield
            where the crack appears
                and youre watching it ripple out
                            right
                    before it
                            shatters

vivienne
what if i came to california too

theres this school
calarts

derek
what about it

vivienne
i got in
as a photography major

derek
your mom would never let you

vivienne
its not her choice

derek
are you kidding
you have to sneak out of the house to see me
almost a full
grown-up adult
and she dictates every single little thing you do
she would never let you go

vivienne
its my choice

derek
shes not going to pay for it
youll never be able to afford it

vivienne
i have a full scholarship
i can do it without her

derek
youre going to defy your mother
YOU
vivienne woods
your father is one thing
he might let you go
but your mother
youd break before your mouth found the words

vivienne
i love you

silence
silence
silence
pieces of the old chinese song fill the space

vivienne
will you say something

derek
thank you

vivienne
i dont
i wont
i dont think you should say it back if you dont mean it
but
but
but
ive been saying it to you
and every time you say thank you
it just
like you know
hurts or something
and im trying to like
i dont know
figure out my life or whatever
and im trying to make these really hard choices
and i dont want to come to california just for you
but i mean if you dont love me then i should just know
because these choices will affect
like the rest of my life
              he grabs her and kisses her

derek
do you remember
when we first met
i said
i said
im japanese

vivienne
yea

derek
i looked at you and said

i know you see a black man
and you think american
or african american
but i was raised in japan
my whole life
so even though you look at me and see this one thing
and categorize it in your mind in this box that you understand
in this box that you are used to
it doesnt actually fit there
think of me as japanese
culturally
mentally
emotionally
think of me as japanese
that is my language
i am japanese

                    he says a japanese phrase

vivienne
what does that mean

derek
ive never said i love you to anyone
in japanese there is no real equivalent anymore
it seems like something old fashioned that people from the past would
    say to each other
its not something i am used to

                    she kisses him

vivienne
will you say it
just so i know
so i understand
my way

derek
i love you

vivienne
i love you too

                    a moment

derek
thats a beautiful song

vivienne
they've been here since before i existed
its a very old song

> *they listen for a moment*

vivienne
i want to go to california

derek
but your mother will never let you

vivienne
ive already turned down harvard

> *they hold hands and listen to the music*
> *after a moment*
>> *they get up and go*
> *as they go*
>>> **vivienne** *stops in front of the statue and looks at it*
>> *she drops some change into its hat and walks away*
>>> *after a moment*
> *the statue COMES TO LIFE*
>> *he moves*
>>> *he looks around*
> *and then . . .*
>> *he follows them*

scene.

>> *a record store*
>>>> *well say its OTHER MUSIC on 4th st and lafayette*
>> *hipsters*
>>> *musicians*
> *the kind of people that listen to music on vinyl are hanging out looking at records*

>>> **luke** *is trying to fit in perusing around the store*
>>>> *he is young, gay, and asian*
>>>>> *good looking*
>> *cool*
>>> *but not as cool as he wants to be*
>>>>> *he picks up a record and flips it over*

> *after a moment*
>>> **kaelan** *comes up to him*
>>>>> **kaelan** *is actually cool*
>>>>>> *or*
>>>> *hes probably "as cool" as* **luke** *is*
>>>>> *but hes not trying to be more than he is*
>>>> *hes comfortable in his skin*
>>>>> *scruffy, white t, skinny jeans, boots, you get the deal*

kaelan
thats a really good record
definitely one of my favorites

luke
ive never heard it

kaelan
love will tear us apart

luke
which one is that

kaelan
oh come on man

>>> **kaelan** *sings the song*

kaelan
when routine bites hard
and ambitions are low

and resentment rides high
but emotions wont grow
                    but **luke** *isnt getting it*
            kaelan *is trying really hard, but like cool you know*
                        its totally cute

kaelan
and were changing our way
taking different roads
NO?

luke
um

kaelan
love
love will tear us apart again
                    is **luke** *embarrassed a little?*
                                are people watching?

luke
oh yea!

                    but he doesnt really get it

kaelan
love
love will tear us apart again

luke
i saw the movie

kaelan
control

luke
yea
so i thought i should get it
and like listen to them

kaelan
that record changed my life

luke
cool
ill definitely listen to it

kaelan
do you come in here a lot

luke
no
this is my first time
im meeting my friends for tai chi around the corner but im
im early

kaelan
you do tai chi
thats awesome

luke
wait
are you
youre kaelan burke

kaelan
yea

luke
luke wood

                                     kaelan *doesnt know who that is*

luke
you graduated two years ago from stuy

kaelan
yea

luke
i was a freshman

kaelan
oh rad

luke
i thought you like went to stanford or something

kaelan
i did
for a while
but it wasn't
it wasn't for me you know

luke
you dropped out of stanford

kaelan
yea

luke
why
who does that

kaelan
i do
it just didnt make sense to spend all that money on something i wasn't
    totally happy with

luke
what did your parents say

kaelan
they were whatever about it
less money for them to spend

luke
crazy

kaelan
no big deal

luke
are you still dating that chick
lisa or whatever

kaelan
nah
we broke up a while ago
didnt really fit
what about you
are you seeing anyone

luke
i dont really like any of the guys at my school

kaelan
oh right on
im sort of between things right now
trying to figure out what fits

luke
oh
oh
yea
thats cool

kaelan
were too young to be settling down and making like permanent choices
   you know

luke
sure
so what
like what are you up to
since youre not in school

kaelan
this

luke
what

kaelan
i work here

luke
at the record store

kaelan
yep

luke
whoa

kaelan
what

luke
you work in a record store
like in a john hughes movie

kaelan
yea well
someone has to i guess

luke
right
i just
i guess i never thought about it
who actually works in a record store

kaelan
i do

luke
right
yea
thats awesome

kaelan
i love music

luke
are you in a band
tell me youre in a band

kaelan
guilty

luke
guitar

kaelan
drums

luke
youre like so relaxed though

kaelan
probably cuz i take it out on the drums

luke
definitely

kaelan
i think that customer needs something
he like keeps eyeing me
i cant tell if he actually needs help or if hes just eye fucking me

luke
probably both
id—id fuck you—
id—id eye fuck you

kaelan
you just said that

luke
yep
so i got to get to tai chi

kaelan
you want that record

luke
do you have it on cd

kaelan
dont get that shit on cd man
its joy division

luke
i dont have a record player

kaelan
but you were looking at the vinyl section

luke
right
well
i dont have a record player
but
i want to be the kind of guy who does

kaelan
you just said that too

luke
yea well
my sister says im impulsive
its yea
i should go

kaelan
what are you doing later

luke
homework

kaelan
ha
thats cute

luke
you work in a record store
thats cute

> *did this throw* **kaelan** *off his game or did he find it cute?*

luke
im gonna meet my friends in columbus park in chinatown
its a couple blocks from my house
so we study there

kaelan
oh yea
thats rad
i play basketball there sometimes

luke
cool
maybe ill see you there

        luke *is about to go but then . . .*

kaelan
listen

        kaelan *points up*

luke
what

kaelan
no—
just listen

      and then
the world is filled with the sound of joy divisions "love will tear us apart"
it EXPLODES into a technicolor dream

      and suddenly
they are in the pop music video
of
their lives

scene.

> **joanna davidowitz** *sits in her office*
> *floor-to-ceiling windows*
> > *certificates and plaques on the walls*
> > *this office is in a building run by a huge corporation*
> > > *were talking global engineering*
> *you can see the best view of manhattan from this office*

> > > > *shes on the phone*

joanna
send them all to china
ive been saying it for years
we need our strongest out there
its time
forgive me if its un-AMERICAN to say that
but seeing as how were a capitalist society
and this
this is a capitalist company
it seems almost un-AMERICAN to do the opposite

> > > *there is a knock at the door*
> > *she keeps talking*

joanna
exactly
im with you bob

> > *another knock*

joanna
come in
ned
oh hes fine
but hes not our man
josh is our man
yes
he has his priorities in the right place

> > **tin wong** *opens the door and approaches*
> > > *very mildly*
> > > > *maybe head bowed*
> > > *hes terrified of interrupting*
> > > > *he is well dressed—*
> > > > *but not too well dressed*

> *and well mannered*
> *he blends in*
> **joanna** *motions for him to sit down*
> *he does so*

joanna
right right
he has no family
moving him will be easy and efficient
my two favorite things
perfect
perfect
ill make the call right now
whats that bob
exactly
talk soon
ciao
tin
what can i do for you

tin
i know youre busy

> *a moment*

joanna
so get to it

tin
i wanted to talk to you about brett phillips

joanna
what about him

tin
the promotion

joanna
hes going to be out celebrating all night

tin
i know you have your reasons for making choices the way you do

joanna
thats right
nothings an accident here

tin
and i dont want to overstep my boundaries

joanna
then dont

tin
i would never want to do that
i love my job
i am happy here
this is the best place to be an engineer

joanna
we think so too
so im glad to hear you feel that way too tin

tin
but i am here because

joanna
because

tin
because i have been with this company for five years

joanna
and they've been a great five years

tin
they have
im not complaining

joanna
good to hear

tin
and in those five years ive seen my colleagues rise to higher ranks
in those five years my counterparts have risen to better and higher jobs
i now have superiors who have spent less than half the time i have at this
    company

joanna
so whats the point

tin
i thought this was going to be my time
brett phillips has only been here two years jo
the other night in bed—

joanna
i told you never to talk about that here

tin
im sorry
but if im good enough for you in bed
i should be good enough here

joanna
youre treading a fine line

tin
just listen to me please
the other night
you said you would consider me

joanna
i thought you were joking

tin
why would i be joking
what can brett phillips do that i cant as well
why would you not consider me for this promotion

joanna
they would laugh
if i even suggested it in the meetings
they would laught at the thought of—
an outburst

tin
the thought of what
im smarter than half the people youve promoted before me
im a harder worker
im diligent
im here on time
i work extra hours
i listen and i am attentive
why am i not in charge now
explain it to me
im fucking tired—

joanna
DONT TALK TO ME THAT WAY

silence
    silence
        silence
    hes never spoken to anyone this way

tin
im sorry
im exhausted

joanna
you dont have what it takes

tin
what it takes

joanna
im going to tell you this because i like you
off the record
you are just not a leader
the people who lead these companies are tigers
they are tigers that make even the most powerful tremble before them
they are people to be feared
they are people you do not cross
they are people whose eyes you do not look at directly
like the sun because they might burn you with one simple gaze
like medusa because you might become nothing but stone in front of
    them
they command presence
they command respect
does this sound like you

tin
i mean

joanna
DOES
THIS
SOUND
LIKE
YOU

tin
i work hard

joanna
i didnt think so

tin
are you saying this is where im going to be the rest of my life

joanna
most of the company doesnt even know your name
and the ones who do
dont even say it right
they call you TIM
TIM
and you never even correct them

tin
i didnt want to insult them

joanna
being what you are is fine tin
youre not a tiger
youre a worker bee
but youre an excellent worker bee
be proud of that

tin
so this is the end of the line for me

joanna
no one takes you for a leader tin
you dont speak up in meetings
you dont present new ideas

tin
thats because i listen
that is how i show respect

joanna
well your respect is not getting you anywhere

tin
so this is it
this is what the company thinks

joanna
im telling you as a friend
okay
i have a meeting i need to get to

tin
okay

joanna
ill see you tonight

tin
sure

joanna
off you go

tin
joanna

joanna
yea

tin
thank you for your honesty
the sound of a bomb on the verge of going off

scene.

columbus park
a small boom box plays soothing music
calming sounds
we can still hear pieces of new york breathing
alive
luke *and* **koren**
stand facing each other in a circle
koren *is pretty cool, sort of spastic and ADD breaking into song*
whenever bored
shes in more practical yoga sweats and a t-shirt
luke*, the ringleader, stands shirtless*
they are doing tai chi
even though theyve done it before
they dont REALLY remember what theyre doing
right now theyre doing the warm-up exercise making fists and hitting their
sides
oh yea, theyre high school juniors
and they speak like rapid fast likeyouhavenoideayouknowwhatimsaying

koren
whys this bitch always late

luke
always

koren
always

koren
ohmygod luke
my aunt totally tried to add me on facebook today

luke
NO
what did you do

koren
not confirm her
obvi

luke
i confirm everyone

koren
even people you dont know

luke
yea
all press is good press

koren
what about your parents

luke
neither of them is on facebook
thank god

koren
yea its weird

luke
totally weird

> *a moment*
> > *and then*
> > **brandi** *lazily walks in*
> > > *shes in very form-fitting pink tights and a cut-off shirt*
> > *headband*
> > > *i dont think she knows this madonna look*
> > > *was vintage and cool five years ago*
> > *now its come and gone again—but shes often late to the party*

brandi
why arent you wearing a shirt

luke
i forgot my other shirt at home and i dont want to get this one all sweaty

brandi
i dont believe you

luke
shut up brandi
its not like hes fat or anything

brandi
fuck off koren
nobody asked you
hes just trying to show off

luke
so what if i am

koren
its not a bad view

luke
thanks koren

koren
youre welcome baby

brandi
you guys disgust me

luke
quit being a bitch and breathe out your mouth

koren
i always forget to breathe

brandi
who are you showing off for

luke
none of your business

brandi
tell me

luke
no

koren
dont tell her luke

brandi
koren

koren
its more fun to watch her squirm

brandi
no fair you guys
this isnt how bffs treat each other

luke
nope

brandi
come on please

luke
you always get all jealous and shit

koren
mad jealous

brandi
not true

luke
you get all competitive
and like try to take things that arent yours

koren
yea like a vulture

brandi
a what

luke
a vulture
you know a bird

brandi
i know what a vulture is you bitch
why am i like a vulture

koren
cuz your always like scavenging
like taking other peoples shit
and like saying its yours
like making it yours
or something

brandi
nah ah

koren
like the time you tried to tell everyone you discovered patti smith
even though everyone had already been reading that book

brandi
i gave that book to daniella

koren
right
or like how i got my nails done at that place in soho and then the next
    day you did too

brandi
were bffs
imitation is the biggest form of flattery

luke
except when you take credit for it

koren
or like how you tried to lay claim on derek

brandi
fuck you

luke
shouldnt have brought that up k

koren
ohmygod its been like a year
like get over it already

brandi
that bitch stole my man

koren
except she didnt

brandi
she totally did
at the end of last year
right before summer
this bitch vivienne
this bitch VI-VI-ENNE
didnt even look up
didnt even bat an eye
this bitch
my bff
my best friend forever
your sister
totally hears me
LUKE

luke
what

brandi
you were there

luke
she did

brandi
i did

see
i did

koren
its not stealing if it aint yours
he picked her

brandi
koren
you are working my last nerve
i cant believe youre going to take her side over mine

koren
i didnt pick no one
im here arent i

brandi
alright switzerland

koren
youre just mad vivienne won
she always wins

brandi
bitch i will shank you

koren
your tiny white ass
please

luke
should we do some stretches now

koren
you guys
i dont think this works very well

brandi
yea
i dont feel centered or at peace or anything

luke
thats cuz you bitches havent stopped talking since we started
youre supposed to be quiet

they are quiet for a moment
and then
    koren *sings a line or two from a contemporary song*
its like rihanna or alicia keys or janet
maybe shes really really old school giving you some whitney houston
shes really, really good

luke
silence koren

koren
sorry
sometimes it just happens
the song is in me you know
and it needs to come out
it begs to be heard
i cant ignore the impulses

luke
will you just control yourself

koren
ill try
ill shut up

luke
good

koren
but only if you promise

luke
promise what

koren
to take me to that bar
where they have the karaoke

luke
winnies

koren
yes

luke
koren again

koren
please
i cant help myself

luke
i dont know

koren
come on

luke
fine

koren
thank you boo boo

> *a moment of silence*
> *and then it is broken*
> **brandi** *sings a piece of a song BADLY*
> *and you know, its something like totally lame*
> *like kesha or taylor swift*
> *or like nicki minaj*

luke
what. the. fuck.
i will choke you in your sleep
> *she doesnt stop*

luke
brandi
BRANDI

koren
this bitch has gone up and lost her mind

luke
BRANDI
> *she stops*

luke
thank you

brandi
tell me who it is
tell me who it is
tell me who it is
come on
tell me who youre showing off for

tellmewhoitis
tellmewhoitis
tell me who it is and ill stop
ill stop
ill stop

luke
FINE
its kaelan

brandi
KAELAN
WHOS KAELAN

luke
shut up brandi
dont yell his name
why dont you fuckin tweet about it
jesus

brandi
sorry
whos kaelan

luke
graduated two years ago kaelan

brandi
HOT KAELAN

luke
BRANDI

koren
shouldnt have told her

brandi
shut up koren

koren
im just sayin

brandi
you aint saying shit
he is so hot

koren
its all that weight he lost
remember when he used to be fat

brandi
that was a long time ago

luke
i dont know
hes like so confident
like hes got swagger or something

brandi
yea i guess so
id toss it at him

koren
see
you shouldnt have said shit

brandi
what
its not like he can have him or anything
hes straight

luke
well

brandi
WELL
what have you heard

luke
i thinks hes like bi now
or something
i dont know

brandi
thats so cool
like me

koren
you are not bi brandi

brandi
except for that time we hooked up

koren
we didnt hook up
we made out
and it was once
when we were drunk

brandi
whatever
youre so narrow minded
trying to box me in
telling me i cant be who i am

luke
youre not bi brandi

brandi
you dont know
you dont know anything
my identity is fluid
i am discovering who i am

koren
more like ripping off everyone else

brandi
what bitch

koren
fine brandi
youre bi
well get you a sticker

brandi
lick my cooch

koren
you wish

brandi
so how do you know

luke
i dont know
i think he was maybe flirting with me
at the record store

brandi
wait
i thought he went to stanford
this is so confusing

luke
he dropped out
moved back
and now works at the record store

brandi
people dont work in record stores

koren
he does

brandi
thats like gross or something

luke
whats gross

brandi
you cant like date somebody who works in a record store
fuck him maybe
but date
no
thats like
so
thats like not classy
thats like
so lower class
youre like better than that
might as well date someone who works at fucking starbucks or
   something

luke
shut up brandi

koren
yea brandi
youre being a total bitch

brandi
im just saying what were all thinking
he works in a record store
he cant support you
hes not going anywhere
hes like unmotivated and apathetic

luke
shut up brandi
youre a spoiled white bitch
whose mom pays for everything
you can only afford to talk shit

cuz your mom wipes your ass for you with money
dont judge him
what do you know
youve never had a job
youve never worked for anything
you dont know
youre just like spoiled and mean

brandi
i volunteer at the shelter with my mom on weekends

luke
big fuckin whoop
want a medal

brandi
im just saying

luke
and how do you know hes unmotivated
he wants to be a musician

brandi
he and every other bitch in brooklyn
might as well date some broke actors who serves tables

luke
thanks for the support

brandi
im just looking out for you boo boo
you know that

                    a moment

luke
i know

brandi
i love you

luke
sorry i called you a spoiled white bitch

brandi
its okay
i am

luke
im a spoiled white bitch too

brandi
only half
so he flirted with you

luke
yea i think so
and then

brandi
what

luke
i like did research
i like asked around about him

koren
girl you are moving quick

luke
so i heard

brandi
what
what

luke
i dont know
i just heard that like when he drinks
he gets like more "open" or something

brandi
SEE
like me
i am bi
ohmygod
drinking makes you bi

koren
shut up brandi

brandi
so what are you gonna do about it

luke
about what

brandi
kaelan duh

luke
nothing

brandi
what do you mean nothing

luke
im like shy okay
im like shy and shit
leave me alone

brandi
you gotta toss it at him
dont be a pussy

luke
fuck you brandi

brandi
fine
if you dont
then i will

koren
THIS TRICK
luke didnt i say
what did i say

brandi
what
if hes not gonna do anything about it
he'll just end up like wasted unused goods
and thats like lame

koren
five minutes ago he wasnt shit
and now hes unused goods

luke
shut up shut up
shut up
hes here
hes here
and hes like looking
hes like looking over here
do the next move

> *they all awkwardly move into a different stretch*
> *or side*
> *they all*
> *end up going*
> *in different*
> *directions*

luke
fuck
we look like morons
oh shit
oh shit
oh shit oh shit oh shit

koren
what

brandi
what

koren
what

luke
hes coming over here

koren
shit

brandi
fuck

luke
act cool act cool

> **kaelan** *approaches them*
> *hes wearing skinny jeans and boots*
> *white t . . . maybe a black henley*

kaelan
what are you guys doing

luke
tai chi

kaelan
cool

brandi
yea
lukes like people do it you know
so we took a class

kaelan
your people

brandi
the koreans

luke
were chinese brandi

brandi
but the karaoke bar

luke
is korean
but im chinese

brandi
how was i supposed to know

luke
never mind

koren
its really cool
it like makes your body feel good
im koren
this is brandi
worked out and stuff
but like puts you at peace
right guys

brandi
totally

luke
at peace
right

kaelan
looks cool

luke
you should try it sometime

kaelan
yea maybe
ive been working out more

luke
yea
i noticed
we noticed

brandi
its been a long time
you look really good

koren
BRANDI

kaelan
thanks
youre looking pretty good too

brandi
thanks

luke
thanks

kaelan
oh
you too
brandi

awkward

koren
so do you have any plans tonight

kaelan
me

koren
yea
friday night

kaelan
thinking of going to a movie

koren
lukes having people over at his house

brandi
you are

koren
yea

luke
totally
you should come

kaelan
yea

koren
lukes got beer and everything

brandi
you do

luke
i do

koren
you should definitely come over

kaelan
sounds like a plan

luke
awesome
yea
great
ill facebook you

kaelan
ill see you tonight

and hes off

luke
oh my god

brandi
oh my god

koren
oh my god
i am like the best wing woman ever

brandi
you are so totally getting laid tonight

luke
fuck
what am i gonna do
i dont have beer at my house

koren
i can steal a six-pack from my parents

brandi
is that enough beer for all of us

koren
were not going brandi

brandi
why not

koren
do you wanna be a cock block

brandi
oh yea right

luke
but what am i gonna tell kaelan

koren
ouch

luke
what

she coughs

koren
i think i have a cold

luke
what about brandi

brandi
yea what about brandi

koren
shes coming over and feeding me chicken soup

brandi
i am

koren
you are
we can have our own six-pack

luke
nice

brandi
nice

koren
good session

luke
yea
tai chi is awesome

scene.

>   *the family living room*
>   *it is a well-appointed apartment*
>   *clean, classy, upscale, tasteful*

>   **vivienne** *is playing the violin*
>   *its beautiful but sad and harsh*
>   *she plays for a few minutes*
>   *and then*
>   *there is a knock at the door*
>   *she doesnt hear it at first*
>   *and then the knock happens again*
>   *still she doesnt hear it*
>   *and then the knock gets louder*
>   *and louder*
>   *and LOUDER*
>   *startled*
>   *she scratches on the violin*
>   *she sets it aside and goes to the door and opens it*
>   *the* **old-fashioned traveling salesman** *stands at the door*
>   *he is tall, lean, well dressed and dapper*
>   *this man*
>   *well he is not your everyday* **traveling salesman**
>   *he is wearing a dark purple suit*
>   *more opening night at the met ball than salesman*
>   *he wears fabulous shoes—*
>   *maybe they are suede or have a heel*
>   *his hair is slicked back and he has a huge grin on his face*
>   *in his hand he holds a beautiful, classy suitcase with an imprinted*
>   *logo on it*
>   *this shit is fierce and high-class emerald city style*
>   *everything about this man is precise*
>   *his movement, his speech, his expressions are all purposeful and flawless*
>   *he does this a lot*
>   *and more importantly*
>   *he does it well*

vivienne
can i help you

traveling salesman
good evening
im here to see miss wood

vivienne
she is still at work

traveling salesman
i am not here to see julie ann wood
on the faculty of so and so university
whose train arrives in precisely thirty-three minutes and fifty-two seconds
i am here to see miss vivienne wood

vivienne
there must be some mistake

traveling salesman
there are never any mistakes miss

vivienne
did the doorman let you up

traveling salesman
thats right

vivienne
he didnt buzz me

traveling salesman
he was expecting me
im making house calls in the building today
door to door
we are part of the same union your doorman and i

vivienne
okay

traveling salesman
may i come in

vivienne
my mother isnt here

traveling salesman
im here for you

vivienne
i think theres been—

traveling salesman
we never make mistakes
vivienne wood
middle names west
mother had an affinity for the designer
slid into a swarm of bees on your fourth birthday
at the park not knowing they would not be happy about it
you still remember those stings dont you
i have in my records that you love elephants
have always wanted to get lost in a jungle on safari
dear girl
the violin is like nails on a chalk board to you
and you dream of enjoying juicy mangos on a summer day far from here
but a great journey still needs to happen before that can occur
we
make
no
mistakes
may i come in
i have another appointment shortly

vivienne
sure

he comes in

traveling salesman
my name is

> *but whenever he says his name all we hear is static*
> *or an old song*
> *or a sharp chord*
> *or silence*
> *even though he is clearly saying it*

traveling salesman
of the old league of traveling salesman

vivienne
excuse me

traveling salesman
miss

vivienne
i didnt catch your name

traveling salesman
my name is

and it happens again

traveling salesman
of the old league of traveling salesman

vivienne
thats odd

traveling salesman
ah yes
as time moves forward things begin to change
new things replace old things
we at the old league believe in direct connection
high-quality service
and personal warnings

vivienne
warnings

traveling salesman
i am here today to talk to you about life insurance

vivienne
life insurance

traveling salesman
you are repeating almost everything i am saying miss
are you some kind of parrot

vivienne
no

traveling salesman
didnt think so
carrying on then
i am here to talk to you about coming up with the best plan for you
it is smarter to purchase these plans sooner than later

vivienne
i dont need life insurance

traveling salesman
everyone needs life insurance

vivienne
i think this is something my parents would take care of

traveling salesman
it is not something to be done by parents im afraid
the commitment and the purchase price need to be settled on
and arranged by you alone
you and your insurance agent
me

vivienne
i think ill talk it over with my parents and contact you later

traveling salesman
im afraid it doesnt work that way
we travel you see
and once i leave
i might not be able to come back
not for a long
long time miss
and by then
well
by then it could be too late
something could have happened by the time i get around

vivienne
happened
what could have happened

> *as the list grows he gets more and more menacing*
> *more manic*
> > *like the seams are falling apart*

traveling salesman
your heel could break sending you plunging down a metal staircase
    snapping your neck
some petty little creature of the night could come out of the darkness
trying to steal your purse and take you away with it
a meteorite could crash through that window tainted with a chemical
turning you into a monster
a tiny little needle could take arms against you and sew you into the
    bottom of the past
left could turn into right
water could become fire and east could become west
car accident
dog bite
snake bite

food poison
blood poison
cancer
crabs
syphilis
a thousand little things could happen right outside that door miss
be smart
invest in your future
protect yourself against life

vivienne
i dont understand
>   *he suddenly becomes cool, calm, and collected*

traveling salesman
life miss
many things could happen at any single moment
we are here to protect you against them
for the right price

vivienne
please get out

traveling salesman
im only trying to help you miss
name the right sacrifice
find the right price
its how life works
in order to get something
you must invest something

vivienne
thank you for stopping by
but i dont need your help

traveling salesman
trust me
you do
for whats coming

vivienne
whats coming

traveling salesman
the future miss
life

vivienne
id like you to go now please

traveling salesman
very well

he gets up and walks to the door

vivienne
sorry
thank you for stopping by

traveling salesman
miss

vivienne
yes

traveling salesman
it is you who is going to be sorry
please take this
my card
most likely
the next time i see you
the price will be too high

she does so

vivienne
thank you

traveling salesman
good evening miss

vivienne
good evening

and he vanishes

scene.

a karaoke bar—winnies
low, red lighting
sort of dingy, sort of campy, sort of hilarious
luke, **brandi**, *and* **koren** *sit at a booth*
sounds of really bad karaoke in the background

luke
thanks for the six-pack koren

koren
of course
youre my bitch
you know id pull through

brandi
why do we always have to come here

koren
cuz its hilarious
and im always the best singer in the room

luke
koren is it your turn yet

koren
im next

luke
good i have to go home soon

koren
for kaelan

luke
for kaelan

koren
for kaelan

brandi
did you guys see alicia ross today
she was all flirting with Brandon
wearing that tiny little scarf things as a dress
doesnt she know
she doesnt even like fit into it

her tits all popping out
like what a skank right
i heard that shes like telling people that she wants to go to prom with him
that shes hoping that he'll ask her
like yea right
like yea fucking right
like he would ever ask her out
like she would ever look good with him
like people would ever believe that they like belong or whatever
some people
some people have no perspective outside of themselves
some people just cant see what everyone else can
fucking alicia ross
and brandon
yea right
yea fucking right
im going to prom with him
not her
not her
shes all
shes all
shes all trying to get in my way
i took care of it
i took care of it
bitch had it coming

luke
what did you do

brandi
did you hear she got herpes from that dude she was fucking from queens
fucking queens

koren
what dude

brandi
you know what dude
this is why you dont fuck dudes from queens

luke
she was fucking some dude from queens

brandi
yep

koren
alicia ross
really
i coulda sworn she was all prudish and shit

brandi
nope

koren
wow
you coulda fooled me

luke
alicia ross
herpes
rough

brandi
and that ladies is how you start a rumor
that is how you take a bitch down

koren
are you serious

brandi
once you put it out there
you cant take it back
people will believe anything

koren
you are so cray cray sometimes
on the real real
cray cray
                    someone calls **korens** *name: KORn*

koren
oh its my turn!
im next
its koREN
                    koren *goes up to the microphone*

luke
seriously b
you can be so fucked up sometimes

brandi
dont give me that look

dont judge me
now im a bitch
i wasnt a bitch when i took down marc foster for calling you a faggot last
    year
cuz you were too much of a bitch to do it yourself
thats the difference between you and i luke
i always gotta do the dirty work
the rest of you just stand aside and reap the benefits
and where were you when everyone was a bitch to me before
in kindergarten when sarah fogel called me a fat cow
or when lauren weems spit in my face
or when jake nguyen told everyone i gave bad head
i dont remember where you were
keeping your distance
well you know what
im not at the bottom anymore luke
im not
im not
ive clawed my way to the top
and im staying up here
and im not feeling bad about it
not one bit
NOT
ONE
BIT

luke
okay

brandi
thats what i thought

> *she giggles and kisses his cheek*
> *and then* **koren** *is on the mic*

koren
this song is for my bffs brandi and luke

> **brandi** *and* **luke** *cheer*
> **koren** *starts to sing* "*i will always love you*" – *whitney houston version*
> *or maybe its* "*i have nothing*"
>> *either way*
> *its serious*
> *but just when the song is about to climax*
>> *there is a*

BLACKOUT
a few gasps and "whats going on" and "boos" are heard

koren
is this another blackout
mother fucking new york city
whys shit always breaking down on me

scene.

> **luke**, **kaelan**, *and* **vivienne** *sit on the floor of lukes room*
> *he has posters of new order on his wall*
> *joy division and the strokes*
> *maybe the breakfast club or st. elmos fire*
> *his room is pretty organized*
> *books, records, everything is meticulous*

> *they are playing liars dice*
> *they shake the cups*
> *SLAM!*
> *they laugh*
> *they go around*
> *maybe twice if its fast*

vivienne
okay guys
this has to be the last round for me

luke
come on you owe me

kaelan
but were having so much fun

vivienne
i have to talk to mom

kaelan
hey
maybe we can crack open some of those beers you mentioned
and listen to music or
something

vivienne
what beers

luke
kaelan

kaelan
oh shit sorry
was that
was that
should i have kept my mouth shut about that

vivienne
YOU HAVE BEER UP HERE

luke
keep your voice down

vivienne
its against the law

kaelan
i brought them over

vivienne
what

kaelan
yea i

vivienne
i thought you said he—

kaelan
no i did
and asked him to stash it

vivienne
luke youve been drinking

luke
youre making me look like an asshole viv

vivienne
well you are an asshole

luke
i cover for you all the time

vivienne
yea and youre a dick about it

luke
please viv

kaelan
be cool viv
come on
we wont go out
were not cruising around and doing shit
well be up here

just listening to music
being chill
no big deal
nothings going to happen

vivienne
kaelan

luke
please viv

mouthing just to her:

luke
(dont ruin this for me)

vivienne
alright fine

kaelan
awesome

luke
thanks
thanks

vivienne
but if you get caught
i didnt know anything about it

kaelan
scouts honor

vivienne
i cant believe im doing this

she leaves

kaelan
dude that was so close
i almost blew it

a moment

kaelan
you wanna put on a record or something

luke
i dont have a record player remember

kaelan
oh yea
thats right
hold on

> **kaelan** *goes over to a large duffel*
> *and pulls out*
> *an old record player*

kaelan
surprise

luke
are you crazy

kaelan
i got a new one recently
so my old one was just like collecting dust under my bed
it needed a loving home
thought you could have it

luke
youre like
thats like
thanks kaelan

kaelan
and

luke
theres more

kaelan
your first record

> **kaelan** *pulls out the joy division record*

luke
youre really nice
youre thoughtful

kaelan
dont mention it
wanna get the beer while i put this on

luke
yea
okay

kaelan
cool

                    luke *fishes the beer from under his bed*
                              or the closet
                      or the bottom of a drawer
                              does he have anything to open it with?
kaelan *puts on the record*
                    a moment
                                        kaelan *dances to the music*
                              its mellow and cute and cool
luke *just watches him*
              light and shadow and young love fill the air

                    kaelan *pulls out his keys and opens the beers*
              maybe he does the lighter trick

luke
thats cool

kaelan
never seen someone do that before

luke
nope
its a neat trick

kaelan
you aint seen nothing yet
im full of em
cheers
                              they clink bottles and drink

luke
sorry everyone else isnt here

kaelan
its cool luke

luke
yea

kaelan
yea

luke
good

kaelan
so thats cool that your parents are okay with you being gay

luke
yea
theyre
its very strange

kaelan
what is

luke
theyre very progressive
i came out when i was fourteen

kaelan
ballsy

luke
when i told my mom
all she said was
make sure hes successful and will take care of you

kaelan
they sound pretty cool your parents
very modern

luke
my mother is chinese
and my father is from connecticut
oddly enough hes the softer one

kaelan
theyre hard on you

luke
as long as we get straight As
we can do whatever we want

kaelan
my parents dont give a shit what i do

luke
must be nice
that kind of freedom

kaelan
sometimes

sometimes the freedom is nice
sometimes the loneliness can be overwhelming
sometimes not having someone looking over your shoulder

luke
breathing down your neck

kaelan
paying attention to you

luke
controlling every move like a chess game

kaelan
holding your hand through the tough shit

luke
forcing your hand into every choice

kaelan
offering advice to progress in the right direction

luke
telling you there is only one way to live

kaelan
correcting all the mistakes they made by making sure you dont repeat
    them

luke
not letting you breathe

kaelan
making sure you dont drown
i didnt have that
sometimes that
that reminds you that you matter to someone
that someone cares about you and they care about your
your survival

luke
that kind of love comes with a price

kaelan
when you fall

luke
sometimes they dont catch you

kaelan
must be—

>**luke** *kisses* **kaelan**
>>*a brief moment*
>>>*and then* **kaelan** *pushes him away*

kaelan
take it easy

luke
sorry

kaelan
no
its just

luke
what

kaelan
give me some time to breathe

luke
okay

>**kaelan** *pops another beer*
>*raises it to the air in a sign of cheers to* **luke** *who nods his head*
>*and then he swallows*
>>>*one*
>>>>*long*
>>>>>*gulp*

scene.

> **vivienne** *addresses her mother*
> *we dont really see her mother*
> *maybe we just see her shadow on the floor*
> *maybe she and* **vivienne** *stand in silhouette*
> *maybe viviennes mother is a puppet*
> *either way*
> *we do not see her in the flesh*
> *but we hear her breathing*
> *feel her reacting*
> *and i cant say its very nice*

vivienne
mom
okay
mother
i mean
i have to tell you something
its important
i think i know where im going to school
i got in
i got in to
ucla calarts
wesleyan
nyu
dartmouth
amherst
vasser
cal
williams
brown
university of chicago
yes i know
i know you think those are all easy ones
mother i
mother i
i want to go to calarts
i got a scholarship
no its
but its
its very prestigious

its
its what i want
photography
its what i want
what
harvard
yes
i did
i did hear back
i
i
i didnt get in

> *suddenly a terrifying sound*
> *as viviennes mother slaps her across the face*
> *once*
> *then twice*
> *then a third time*
> *then a fourth*
> *silence*
> *silence*
> *silence*
> *then in a raspy, almost inhuman voice*
> *we hear the voice of her mother*

the tiger
how dare you shame me
how dare you shame me

> *and then she slaps her again*
> *she starts to stalk away*
> *a moment*

vivienne
by the way mother
might as well tell you now
because youre such a good mother
your son is upstairs getting drunk underneath your nose
just thought you should know

> *a terrifying growl*
> *and then*
> *a blackout*

scene.

at school
two days later—monday
derek *and* **vivienne** *at school*

derek
i respect my family too much
they are too important to me
i would do anything for them
everything

vivienne
how can you do everything for someone who would turn their back on
    you
in the drop of a hat

derek
its about respect
its about doing whats right
its what i most inherited

vivienne
inherited

derek
each of us is born during the year of a certain animal
and we inherit that animals traits
i was born under the year of the boar
and i am proud of that vivienne

vivienne
what am i

derek
a rat

vivienne
gross
its not a very sexy animal
but neither is a boar

derek
maybe not
but the boar represents strength
unbreakable strength that cannot be overcome
honesty as well

most importantly they are brave
and hate to quarrel

vivienne
i dont believe that
that everyone born the same year has the same qualities
it doesnt make sense

derek
you dont have to believe it for it to be true

vivienne
it doesnt matter
love and respect are not the same thing
i choose love

derek
even if it means sacrificing everything

vivienne
well its done now
she'll never forgive me
my father is disappointed
i can see it in his eyes

derek
she will forgive you
i know it

vivienne
its not her im worried about derek
its me

> *he writes something on her hand*

vivienne
whats that mean

derek
its the kanji symbol for forgiveness

vivienne
by the time she realizes ill be long gone
by the time she realizes itll be too late
ill carry this with me forever

derek
in japanese we have a saying

> *he speaks a japanese phrase*

vivienne
what does that mean

derek
it is better to travel hopefully
than to arrive disenchanted

vivienne
maybe ill leave early
start school in the summer
say so long
shes a beast
teach me another saying

derek
im not a fortune cookie full of cheap wisdom

vivienne
yes you are

derek
you have to earn it then

vivienne
come on
im sad
make me feel better

he kisses her

vivienne
what happened to her to turn her into such a beast
i dont understand

derek
there is no way to understand everything

vivienne
is that another one

derek
no

vivienne
come on
teach me one more

derek
okay
ready

vivienne
ready

> **derek** *speaks a japanese phrase*
> > *it is a like a piece of music that hangs in the air*
> > **vivienne** *attempts to repeat it*
> *close*
> > *they do it together one time*

vivienne
what does it mean

derek
unless you enter the tigers den
you cant take the cubs

scene.

> **luke**
> **brandi**
> *and* **koren**
> *skyping*
> *they each listen to soothing sounds at home*
> *they are in their tai chi outfits*

luke
were sitting there
on my bed
hes had two beers
ive had one
and ive like never had alcohol before
so im like feeling pretty good already
and hes looking at me all like
all like
his smile
and his eyes are like just looking at me
and were laughing cuz were like buzzed
and that song is playing in the background

> *he sings a joy division song*
> *its kinda cliché*
> *then* **koren** *sings the song and its really great*

brandi
i love that song

luke
right
were like
the mood is like
like

brandi
perfect

luke
perfect
and im totally freaking out
and im totally excited
cuz its kaelan burke

and hes this close to me
THIS CLOSE

he demonstrates

brandi
wow
thats hot
thats so hot

luke
and i totally have a boner

koren
you did

luke
totally

koren
like a half
like a little hello chub
like just waking up from a nap
all groggy eyed to say hello
or like for real real
like lets do this

luke
full on jet setter

brandi
whoa
what about him what about him

luke
i mean i dont know

brandi
you didnt touch it

koren
we deliver you the goods
i wrap them up all nice and shiny with a little bow on top
all you gotta do is unwrap it

luke
i mean i was nervous
and i was about to
but i was like scared or whatever

but i was like rubbing his back
his shoulders
and i knew

brandi
oh for sure

koren
yea at this point

luke
and right when im about to
mother
she storms in
she motherfucking
my motherfucking would have left me alone all night had my bitch ass
    sister not punked me
my mother
just barges in

brandi
barges

koren
ive had that happen

brandi
embarrassing

koren
the worst

luke
THE WORST

brandi
then what happens

koren
this is too much

luke
she rips me off him and grabs me by both arms and yells
BEER
BEER
BEER
YOU DARE BRING BEER INTO THIS HOUSE

brandi
oh shit

koren
youre like totes fucked

brandi
FUCKED

koren
did you pee yourself
i would have
i would have totally peed myself

luke
and kaelan
is like on the floor
hes like cowering in the corner or something
and hes all like
its my fault
and like im sorry i didnt know
and im like oh shit oh shit oh shit
i thought she was going to rip my face off
she looked at him and said GET OUT
and like a total
like a total fuckin movie
like some michael bay steven spielberg joint
im like
RUN
like RUN like motherfuckin run
you guys it was the worst
and its all because of fucking vivienne

brandi
told you she was a bitch

koren
she totally hated on you

brandi
ruined your life

koren
her own brother

brandi
thats cold

koren
even i didnt think vivi could get down like that
cock block
just cock destroyed you

luke
thats not all

brandi
no wait
theres more

koren
this is like totally stressful you guys

luke
my mom grounded me

brandi
for how long

luke
one month for each beer that she found

koren
fuck you

luke
fuck me is right

brandi
youre grounded for six months

koren
youre grounded for the whole summer

luke
the whole summer

brandi
so no trip to six flags on my birthday

luke
nope

koren
no going to the museum of modern art

luke
exactly

brandi
no looking at cute boys in tank tops in central park

luke
dont even bring that up

koren
its like were all grounded

luke
no summer romance with kaelan

brandi
this is going to be the worst summer ever

> **brandi** *shuts her music off*
> *silence*
> *silence*

brandi
these sounds are not relaxing

koren
no they are not

luke
i do not feel mellow

brandi
i totally dont feel relaxed
but you know what IS relaxing

luke
what

brandi
payback

scene.

> vivienne *is at home*
> *she is reading*
> *and listening to classical music*
> *a knock at the door*
> *she opens it*
> *the* **traveling salesman** *is back*

vivienne
what are you doing here

traveling salesman
as summer approaches
the end of a season
we thought itd be nice
to sell our insurance for a very special price

vivienne
i said i dont want it

traveling salesman
you dont even know how much it costs

vivienne
why would i want to insure something that is barely worth anything

traveling salesman
we only understand the value of what we have
once weve lost it
we only know the worth of something close to us
when it is gone
vanished into thin air
as if it never existed
you are young and think have little to lose
but that which you most need
you will find is lost when most desired
a few simple pennies
some easy demands
take it from me miss
danger approaches

vivienne
okay
how much will it cost

traveling salesman
not how much
but what

vivienne
okay what

he whispers into her ear

vivienne
no
i would never
i would never do that

traveling salesman
a simple price for what you are insuring

vivienne
get out of my house

traveling salesman
you protect that which does not value you

vivienne
please leave

traveling salesman
dear girl
would he not take this offer
you or your brother
your brother future
thats all im asking
your brother future
before he takes yours
its a simple exchange

vivienne
no
no
no
he wouldnt

traveling salesman
are you sure
are you sure
are you sure
are you sure

are you sure
simple insurance can protect you

vivienne
i am
i am
GET OUT

traveling salesman
suit yourself
dont say i didnt warn you
next time
you wont be able to afford the price
                    and he is gone

scene.

luke *and* **brandi**
they are in viviennes room
koren *keeps watch in the hallway*
shes singing old school janet

luke
hurry up

brandi
are you sure shes not going to catch us in here

luke
korens keeping watch
besides
vivienne likes to take long baths
it allows her to think or something
clear her mind

brandi
i bet shes just touching herself
thats what i do

luke
gross

brandi
im serious

luke
i dont want to think about your vagina
and i certainly dont want to talk about my sisters

brandi
im just saying

luke
can you tell me what were looking for please
what does it look like

brandi
paper you idiot
its a piece of scrap paper

luke
i know its paper

but is it in a notebook
a box
what do girls hide things in

brandi
i feel like
a book

luke
what

brandi
i think she stuck it in a book

luke
shes got a ton of books

brandi
okay let me think
we were
i remember we were in central park
she was studying as usual
and i was making this list right
and i told vivienne
i was like you should make one too
and she was all like no thats so stupid
and i was like no its totally fun and hilarious and like who cares
and she was like no
and finally she stopped studying
she got tired and started reading
she started reading
what the fuck was she reading
atlas fucking shrugged
find atlas shrugged

>   *they go through viviennes books*
>   *there are some on her dresser*
>   *there are some on a little bookshelf mounted on the wall*
>   *there are books on the windowsill*
>   *there are a ton of books*
>   *they dig through them*

luke
i got it

brandi
you did

luke
no wait i cant read
im a moron
keep looking

brandi
no
no
no
no

luke
a giant shakespeare anthology

brandi
fuck that guy
thats like not even english
thats like a whole other language

luke
not this one
no

brandi
found it
found it
i found—

luke
stop screaming
she'll hear you
open the book
open the book

> *she flips through the book until a piece of paper*
> > *falls from the sky*
> > *like really*
> > *not from the book*
> > > *but like magically falls from the sky*
> *like a present*
> > *it floats in a dim red light*
> > > *or purple maybe*
> > *and lands at their feet*
> > > **luke** *grabs it and begins to unfold*

brandi
bingo

> *the sound of something shattering*
> *or the sound of all the air from the world being sucked out*

scene.

> **tin** *appears*
>> *he is in a suit*
>>> *he talks to the audience*

tin
hello
hi
its good to be here
its good to be back at stuy

>> *a long silent moment*

tin
its been ten years since i graduated
so it is an honor to speak to you here today
i know im not kevin mitchell
but as you might have heard he recently became ceo of of
you know
so he had to cancel last minute
and i am
i am his replacement
replace
but
so
thank you principal lee for asking me to come back
for thinking so highly of me
thank
thank you

>> *he pulls out a sheet of paper*

tin
stuyvesant class of 2013
welcome—
WELCOME
to the future
to your future
and what
what a beautiful future it is

>> *he stops*

tin
i had this speech all planned out
i was supposed to come back and tell you how great everything is

how after you leave high school
the world will open up for you
as it did for me
with opportunity
with potential
with potential
all the potential in the world
to change everything
to create
to make a difference
i was supposed to tell you that education is important
that education is everything
that after you go to yale like i did
or princeton or harvard or ucla or stanford
or wherever it is that you decide to go
that everything will open up for you
limitless
limitless
but thats not
thats not what im here to tell you
you see
i recently
i recently quit my job
a job that i had been at for almost a decade
i quit
i quit
my job
i quit my job
i am an american
but i am also asian
the two coexist
right
right
they coexist in me
together
so i thought
but what i learned
tradition
value
respect
silence
these things mean nothing to them

what they value
what we value
these things are not in sync
so what are we working for
who is to change
are we learning the right things
i am smarter than them
i know i am smarter than them
i think i am
i think
i know that if i add this and multiply that and divide it here
a meaning will be derived
but what that meaning does
what it actually means
i cannot understand it
its foreign
what about us
what about you
what about me
what about me
how much longer are we to be silence
tradition is all i know
that is all i know
and it hasnt
its killing me
what i know
what i am
what i do
what i do
what i do
i quit my
i quit my
what am i left with
who am i now

       there is a deafening silence

tin
i thought
i worked so hard
but i wasnt good enough
me
can anyone

can anyone help me
i have nothing
what am i
what
please
please
please
listen
cant you see
anyone

do people begin to boo?
does someone gently try to lead him off stage?
or is it just brutal silence?

tin
please
dont you see
i need help
i am just a man
with so many questions
help me to understand
sorry

blackout

scene.

> **luke** *sits in the living room*
> *he is watching a movie*
> *mommie dearest*
> *we hear a soundbite*
> *THAT iconic scream*
> **vivienne** *comes out of her room*

vivienne
hey

> *silence*

vivienne
im still pretty shaken up about that guy
tin
i feel so sad for him
what do you think happened to him
he went crazy
it was sad right
it was sad
luke
luke
alright
tell mom i went to the park

luke
i dont care

vivienne
ill be back before dinner

luke
nobody cares

vivienne
luke

luke
fuck off

vivienne
dont talk to me that way
i love you

luke
i said
FUCK OFF

vivienne
i made a mistake
we all make mistakes
someday you will too

luke
youll be sorry

vivienne
i already am

luke
you dont know how sorry youre going to be

vivienne
there will be other boys

luke
not like this one

vivienne
let me give you some advice—

luke
youre only a year older than me vivienne

vivienne
trust me it makes a difference

luke
tell somebody who cares

vivienne
alright
ill be back later

luke
I DONT CARE

she leaves
he pulls out the note and looks at it
there is a knock at the door
he stuffs the note back in his pocket
another knock
he opens the door

luke
I SAID NO ONE CA—

> *but its not* **vivienne**
> *its the* **traveling salesman**

luke
sorry i thought you were

traveling salesman
good evening my name is

> *but all we hear is static*
> *or an old song*
> *or a sharp chord*
> *or silence*
> *even though he is clearly saying his name*

traveling salesman
of the old league of traveling salesman
and i am here with a very special offer for a mister luke wood

> *he smiles*

scene.

> *the* **traveling salesman** *appears in spot*
> *he speaks to the audience*

traveling salesman
we live in troubling times
times that will only get more troubling
we tried to warn you
to slow you down
to tell you to stop
but you wouldnt listen would you
no
you wouldnt
so now were here to make you listen
to remind you of all the things of which you are capable of
to show you what it is that you have done
and let me remind you
what you have done
not what we have
> *he looks at his watch*

traveling salesman
oh
i think its showtime
youre on kid

> *he points at* **luke**
> *who speaks to the audience*

luke
so if everyone hasnt heard yet
im grounded for the next six months
why
because vivienne decided to rat me out
and tell my parents
about the six-pack of beer i was hiding in my room
my mom is asian
and all of you know
that asian parents
are fucking strict
so six cans equals six months of being grounded
little over the top
not if your parents are asian

and your sister is a filthy bitch
since all i can do
and all ill ever do for the next five and a half months
involves sitting on the computer all day
i thought id get a little revenge today
everyone out there thinks my sister is such a sweet and innocent girl
but a few days ago
i decided to go treasure hunting in her room
with an unnamed friend
who my sister has also fucked over
and found a little something special hidden in her closet
this will make the next five and a half months bearable
ladies and gentleman my sister is a whore
i present to you her hook-up list

> *does* **luke** *read this list*
> *maybe the* **traveling salesman** *does*
> *maybe the whole cast does it*
> *maybe various people appear as they are named*
> *maybe we go back in time and see the list being created*
> *or maybe just* **vivienne**
> *reads it alone in the cold cold light*

vivienne
one

adrian matthews
finger me
maybe hj

two

ronnie trent
blow job

three

dang tran
only kiss

four

josh taylor
finger me

hj
blow job
tittie bang
and maybe v-card

five

derek key

blow job

six

kaelan burke
v-card
but people say hes gay

seven

jacob nguyen
only kiss
if he cuts his hair
i might give him a blow job

eight

russel terra
he ate me out
awesome
i want him to make me go O

nine

nick charles
i will do anything he wants
i will do everything he wants
sooooooooooo
HOT

> *silence*
> *silence*

> *silence*
> > *meanwhile*
> > > *the* **traveling salesman** *grins*
> > > > *and grins*
> > > *and grins*
> > *and grins*
> > *and looks at the audience*

traveling salesman
but lets not forget the flurry of responses

1
note to self
do not hook up with vivienne

2
what a whore

3
damn son

koren
oh em
gee

4
this is
so epic

kaelan
you are a dick
but this is so funny
also im not gay

5
holy shit

brandi
hey jacob
if you cut your hair youre getting a bj
hahahahahahha

derek
HOLY SHIT

6
ohem f
g

7
i love facebook

brandi
i knew she was a closet slut

koren
this is so wrong

8
tweeted it

9
instagrammed it

10
hashtag slut

11
she has some bad taste

12
this trick

13
this bitch

derek
luke
i really think you should take this down
this is so wrong on so many levels

14
CALLED OUT

15
this is so fucked-up

16
i second that

17
if i could like this twice i would
                    and then **vivienne** *catches wind*

vivienne
TAKE THIS DOWN NOW
WHAT THE FUCK IS WRONG WITH YOU

luke
what are you gonna do
tell mom and dad that i uploaded your dick-sucking list to facebook
go ahead

18
omg

kaelan
no way

vivienne
EVERYONE DE-TAG YOURSELVES NOW
REMOVE THE TAGS LUKE OR IM GOING TO SERIOUSLY HURT
   YOU
TAKE THIS PICTURE DOWN NOW
PICK UP YOUR PHONE

luke
i heart facebook like you heart cock

> *and then silence*
> > *and everyone is looking at* **vivienne**
> > > *they are surrounding her*
> > > *they are circled around her*
> > *staring*
> > > *and staring*
> > > > *and staring*
> > *and staring*
> > > *and staring*
> > > > *and then*
> > *a stomp*
> > > *stomp*
> > > > *stomp*
> > *something STOMPING towards everyone*
> > > *and then*
> > > > *a GIANT TERRIFYING GROWL*
> > *blackout*

END OF ACT ONE

act two.

scene.

        a sound like something exploding
     a sound like all of the air is being sucked out of the universe
and the characters are all there
    well all of them except for **luke, vivienne,** *the* **traveling salesman** *and* **the tiger**
        they look at the audience
        in the darkness
       and then they EXPLODE into crazy gesture mode
        crazy
           schizophrenic
               fast and overwhelming
and then they all stop
        suddenly
      as if theyve become aware of the audience
as if theyve caught us looking in on them
          suddenly they all say
    "THIS IS HOW YOU WANTED IT"
and then they go away
      they vanish
        and we bleed into:

scene.

> a den like a bombed-out shelter in a jungle
> a window covered in vines
> the sound of waves crashing
> trees and leaves
> decaying
> a window
> out of this window
> in the distance we see water
> this den is both a complete room
> but also architecturally open
> we see the jungle the room is in
> the jungle is all around
> and breaking through

> **vivienne** is in the corner
> cold and sad and broken and alone
> she has been on a very long journey here
> like a great
> big
> long
> fall
> and then **brandi** appears
> she is a vulture . . .
> literally
> she circles around vivienne
> cackling

brandi
poor poor broken thing

vivienne
come to see what youve done

brandi
i can smell it from way up there
the blood
and the fear
the sadness
you reek of it
that stench

its intoxicating

vivienne
havent you done enough

brandi
im still hungry

               brandi *pecks at* **vivienne**

vivienne
get away

brandi
but youre still fresh
all that meat
ripe for the picking
would be a shame to waste

                      brandi *pecks at* **vivienne**
                 vivienne *tries to push her away*
                          but she is too weak

vivienne
what more do you want

brandi
bone
i want to slurp the marrow

                      she slurps

brandi
i want to get to the juicy bits

vivienne
i never did anything to you

brandi
you took away my happiness
you took from me the thing i wanted

vivienne
you can be the smartest
the fastest
the funniest
you can be the prettiest

you can have him
or her
and this and that
take it
its yours
i dont want it

brandi
you dont have to offer them to me
ill take them for myself

vivienne
just let me dwell here in
in in
in
what this is

brandi
oh
youre no fun when you dont struggle
youre weaker than i thought you were
i thought you were my equal
but youre
just
pathetic
and weak
empty hollow eyes
your eyelids sag
to the floor
like your dripping down forever
melting away
a creature made of liquid
drip
drip
drip
plop
plop
plop
a mess of wet
nothingness

vivienne
you dont know whats inside me

you dont know what i am

brandi
i can tell you this
                                    she pecks at **vivienne**
youre not like me
                                            peck
youre not a majestic bird
                                                    peck
there are no strong feathers lining your back
                                                            peck
you were not made to soar
                                                    peck
you were not meant to spread your body in grandeur
                                            peck
seeking
seeking
seeking
the sky
                                            peck
but instead made to be broken
crushed on the ground
                                            peck
i can see you from way up here vivienne
                                                    peck
do you see me
                                                    peck
i am waving
i am waving
i am waving
down to you
from way up here
from way up here
i am waving
from the top
from the top
waving to you
at the bottom
at the bottom
at the bottom
waving to you

peck

peck

peck

but this time

as she goes to peck her

vivienne *grabs* **brandis** *wings*

vivienne
you are no beautiful bird brandi
you are no strong

brandi
let go of me

vivienne
or courageous
or honorable bird

brandi
youre hurting me

vivienne
you are neither song bird nor cardinal
you are no mocking bird or owl

brandi
my wings

vivienne
you dont have the vibrant colors of a flamingo or parrot

brandi
ow

vivienne
you are no raven or condor or eagle or hawk

brandi
ow

vivienne
youre nothing but
a vulture
a filthy
scrap-eating
vulture
a dirty
dishonorable

vulture
i may not be a beautiful winged bird
but at least
at least
i am no vulture

now flit off before i snap off your wings

          vivienne *lets* **brandi** *go*
   the sound of a thunderstorm approaching
     brandi *makes the loud jagged sound of a vulture*
           she flies away
       a little less high than when she came in
  vivienne *is alone*
    she is lost
      and alone
        she starts to sing a song
   the song is current
    some brooklyn hipster song by girls
      or twin shadow
       or the xx
    you know the kind of song
      she sings
  but the song doesnt seem to come out right
    she tries over and over again
she tries again but all that comes out is a cry in a different language
    the cry is like a cough
      she chokes on the words and then quiets down
    confused
      thinking
    until she starts to sing another song
       one that feels familiar
         yet not
  the song is very old
   ancient
    like the one we heard in the park
   an old chinese song
    she sings for a moment
      and then
    derek *wanders in*
    he is
    a BOAR

derek
at the center of the jungle
somewhere deep down and dark
i woke up lost
i woke up twisted and entangled
blurry tongued and bloody eyed
i felt trapped in my body
my own body became my own enemy
feeling unfamiliar
this body that id known so well
this body id known so long
all id known
had turned on me and become something
unrecognizable
like a glove on the wrong foot
like a song with the wrong words kissed into your ears
by someone
by something
you used to know
so i followed the sounds
letting them lead me to a place that felt familiar
only to find
only to find
only to find
you
who are you

vivienne
vivienne

derek
you dont sound like her
you dont look like her

he kisses her

derek
you dont taste like her

vivienne
its me

derek
i dont believe you

vivienne
its still me

its me
its me

derek
things are different here
how odd

vivienne
that list

derek
that list

vivienne
that list
i wrote it a long time ago

derek
a long time ago

vivienne
before you and i even knew each other

derek
before

vivienne
before

derek
before

vivienne
before the idea of you and i was even invented
i was a different person then

derek
a different person

vivienne
just a child

derek
just a child

vivienne
you understand me right

derek
you

vivienne
right

derek
just a child

vivienne
derek

derek
sometimes things get trapped in your head
and no matter how hard you try you cant get them out
yes
no
maybe
right
what
wait

vivienne
i love you

derek
im overwhelmed by feelings
i didnt know i had
like the levee broke and all this stuff is rushing in
but love
isnt one of them

vivienne
you dont mean that

derek
i think i do

vivienne
i didnt know you could be so cold

derek
i didnt know you could be so cheap

vivienne
it was a small thing
i wrote a long time ago
when i was a freshman
just a kid
a childish thing

derek
but right now
it feels like the most important thing in the world
and right now feels like itll last forever

vivienne
nothing lasts forever

a moment

derek
the image i have of you
is seered into my brain
and ill think of it
and live in it
so that next time
i wont be so foolish
i wont be so foolish

he starts to go
a moment

vivienne
derek

he turns around

vivienne
i didnt take you for a coward
i thought you were supposed to be brave
so much for your unbreakable strength

derek
so often things are not what you want them to be
people can be so surprising

and he disappears
after a moment
the sounds of a thunderstorm getting closer
and closer
and closer
vivienne *looks for cover*
and then tropical winds
and rain
and rain
and rain
the **old-fashioned traveling salesman** *appears*
he watches her
he feels sorry for her

traveling salesman
i told you this wouldnt end well for you

vivienne
leave me alone

traveling salesman
im the only friend you got down here

vivienne
friend
i dont even know what that word means
friend
friend
its like metal in my mouth
rotten and poisonous
i choke on the word friend

traveling salesman
you can still get out

vivienne
theres nothing for me back there

traveling salesman
that so juvenile of you

vivienne
well i am
just a juvenile

traveling salesman
you are no kid doll
at least not anymore
youre older now

vivienne
all ive learned
is that in this life
there is no winning
in this life
traps everywhere
giant bear claws meant to snap you in half
no matter what direction you run in
holes everywhere
hidden under leaves
where you cant see

traveling salesman
im going to tell you something
because i like you

vivienne
why

traveling salesman
because i like you

vivienne
why

traveling salesman
cant a person just like another person these days

vivienne
not your kind of person

traveling salesman
ouch
what you have to learn
is very simple
its very american
actually
its not even american
just a fact about the world
are you listening

vivienne
fuck off

traveling salesman
in this life everything comes with a price
everything costs something
if you want anything
you have to give something up
its as simple as that
what are you willing to risk for what you want
what will you sacrifice
evolve
evolve
evolve
youre not a child anymore
you cant have it all
you should have taken my offer

vivienne
i couldnt

traveling salesman
your brother is the reason youre down here

vivienne
well i dont believe in revenge

giant growling sounds are heard in the distance

traveling salesman
suit yourself
this is the last youll see of me

he starts to go

vivienne
wait
what about her

traveling salesman
who knows what she has planned for you
but you have a lifetime to find out

a moment

and then

vivienne
you can have him
whatever he was meant to be
the life he was meant to lead

traveling salesman
im sorry

vivienne
now what

traveling salesman
that deals no longer on the table

vivienne
but what
i thought

traveling salesman
thats the thing about insurance

if you wait
the price can change
your brother already made his own deal with me
hes very impulsive

vivienne
what did he

traveling salesman
oh im sorry
customer salesman privilege
you know how it is

vivienne
so thats it

traveling salesman
im afraid so

vivienne
just me and her then

traveling salesman
well there is

vivienne
what

traveling salesman
no
never mind
i couldnt

vivienne
tell me

traveling salesman
there is another way

he gets close to her and opens his mouth
and then the deafening noise
the static
the overwhelming

vivienne
what if i dont

traveling salesman
its only if
                                she thinks

vivienne
if i accept your proposition

traveling salesman
ill take care of her

vivienne
i accept

traveling salesman
stay still and quiet
and dont say a word

                          he points to another corner
                                  and **luke** *appears*

luke
hello
                      and then the roar of a **tiger**

luke
mom

                  and then all of a sudden
                          stuff
                                    flies
            through
                          the air
                    like its being tossed
            its coming from a dark corner
                    stuff is being flung out the window
                    onto the water below
            shoes
                    books
                              pictures
            sweaters
                                  love
            memories
                    cardboard cutouts
                the stuff that makes a life

luke
mom
mom what are you doing
mom is that my
is that my stuff
what are you doing
what are you doing

> **luke** *sees the* **traveling salesman**
> *maybe he runs to him and grabs his arm*
> *maybe he just tries to wave him down*
> *either way*
> *hes trying to get his attention*
> *desperately*

luke
i thought you were helping me

traveling salesman
i am

luke
but look

traveling salesman
oh im sorry
i have nothing to do with that
not
a
thing

luke
youre leaving

traveling salesman
oh ill be back
to collect
we always do

> *and he vanishes*
> *leaving* **luke** *alone*
> *because thats how it is*
> *isnt it*
> *with insurance*
> *you always forget to protect yourself against*
> *SOMETHING*

and then **luke** *is alone*
and then **the tiger** *growls*
and then **the tiger** *stalks towards* **luke**
the tiger *is limber and beautiful in its haute couture*
it circles around **luke**
it licks its lips

the tiger
you tied the noose around your own neck

she picks up things that matter to him
things that make him who he is

the tiger
your first baby picture

she tears it up and throws it out

the tiger
your favorite blanket

out the window

the tiger
a scrapbook you made for me in first grade

out

the tiger
your house keys

out

the tiger
you favorite book

out

the tiger
i will erase you
and you will no longer exist to me
no longer my son

luke
please dont say that

the tiger
you did this

luke
im sorry

she picks up the joy division record

luke
no
pleaseplease

the tiger
first love
oh this is precious to you isnt it

luke
please

> *she SNAPS it in half*
> *he slides down into the corner*

> *from another part of the stage*
> **vivienne** *watches*
> *and then*
> *just when* **the tiger** *goes to eat* **luke**

vivienne
mother dont

the tiger
ive been waiting for you

vivienne
well im here now

the tiger
do mommy a favor and play her her favorite song wont you

vivienne
mother

the tiger
right over there

vivienne
but

the tiger
NOW

> **the tiger** *throws a glare and a growl her way*
> *it frightens her*
> **vivienne** *walks over to the violin and begins to play*

the tiger
now thats a good girl

> *the violin plays*
> **the tiger** *stalks over to* **luke**
> *she gets closer and closer to him*
> *until he can feel her breath on his skin*

the tiger
what a disappointment you turned out to be
stupid modern american boy
shameless impulsive failure
thats who you are

> **vivienne** *stops playing the violin*

vivienne
thats enough
what about you

the tiger
what about me

vivienne
youre a failure

> *a deep growl*

the tiger
what did you say

vivienne
we could have gotten straight a's
and perfect jobs
the house
and the lawn
the prizes you so adore

the tiger
i wanted people to respect me
to respect you
to respect us

vivienne
i got into harvard mother
but i decided not to go

the tiger
and now youll suffer for it

vivienne
no mother
youre going to suffer
you are
because you failed mother
mother
mother
mother
mother
you FAILED
you dont even have our respect

the tiger
when im done with him
youll be next

>   **the tiger** *makes a giant growl*
>   *like its about to tear* **luke** *to pieces*
>   *and then with all her might*
>   **vivienne** *runs up to* **the tiger**
>   *and smashes the violin over her head*
>   *darkness*
>   *the sounds of the violin being smashed over and over*
>   *and over and over*
>   *and over and over*
>   *as this happens a fucked-up menacing violin song plays*
>   *it reverberates*
>   *it stretches like its being ripped apart*
>   *the rest of the cast appears*
>   *they do their fucked-up gesture dance to the violent sounds*
>   *everything being ripped apart*
>   *chaos*
>   *and frenzy*
>   *they are trying to keep up*
>   *but its all too much*
>   *its all too quick*
>   *and they can barely keep up*
>   *pushing themselves further and further and further*
>   *pushing themselves almost out of their bodies*
>   *trying to push themselves forward*
>   *trying to keep up*
>   *blackout*

END OF ACT TWO

act three.

scene.

ten years later
the sounds of a street in brooklyn
    kaelan *stands in a suit and tie on a tree-lined street*
      he checks his watch
  he takes a seat on a bench looking around
        waiting
   after a moment he looks at his watch again and paces
    he pulls out his cell phone and makes a call

kaelan
hey
its kaelan
its two forty-five
youre fifteen minutes late
our appointment is at three
i told you
i need everything to run smoothly today
text me as soon as you get here
hop in a cab
just get here
okay

    he hangs up the phone
    and looks at his watch again
  after a minute
    luke *casually takes a seat next to him*
      they dont recognize each other
  and then **luke** *checks out* **kaelan**
      and makes the connection

luke
kaelan

kaelan
yes

  a moment where they both awkwardly look at each other

kaelan
luke

luke
hey!
hey
HEY

they hug

kaelan
what are you—

luke
waiting to pick up—

kaelan
you have a kid here

luke
oh no no
not me no
never—

kaelan
no—

luke
a friend
im picking up my friends daughter

kaelan
oh—

luke
yea—

kaelan
oh—

luke
wait do you—

kaelan
no—

luke
no—

kaelan
sort of—

luke
sort of—

kaelan
well were here for an interview

luke
we

kaelan
my son and i

luke
hes—

kaelan
late
i mean
his nanny
shes supposed to meet me here
i was at work
we have a
a you know
an interview thing
at three
so thats why im
yea
you look great

luke
thanks
you too yea
so you have a son

kaelan
yea

luke
wow

kaelan
i know

luke
how old is he

kaelan
four

luke
four
wow
thats
wow
thats amazing
thats
you know
so adult of you

kaelan
i know right
its a
yea
i never thought i was the type
but yea
i guess i am

luke
definitely
definitely
i bet youre a great father

kaelan
do you

luke
you were always so
open

kaelan
right
thanks

luke
nurturing

kaelan
thats sweet

luke
and youre in a suit

kaelan
yea

luke
and tie

kaelan
i know

luke
youre a—

kaelan
doctor

luke
wow

kaelan
its
you know
busy
and you

luke
i
me

kaelan
yea

luke
i work in marketing

kaelan
marketing

luke
you know
thats the
vague
the vague
im a graphic designer

kaelan
right brain

luke
no surprise there

kaelan
yea well

its all the same

luke
so youre married

kaelan
separated

luke
oh okay
sorry to hear that

kaelan
no
its
for the better

luke
yea

kaelan
yea
and you

luke
single
single
single
perpetually single

kaelan
i dont believe it

luke
im emotionally damaged
thats what i tell people

kaelan
so youre normal

luke
i have commitment issues

a phone rings
the ringtone is "love will tear us apart"

kaelan
im sorry
i have to take this

luke
yea sure

kaelan
how far are you guys
okay
fine
yea
thats fine
its okay

> *he hangs up the phone*

luke
everything okay

kaelan
yea

> **luke** *is smiling*

kaelan
what

> **luke** *sings a piece of the old joy division song*
> **kaelan** *laughs*
> *its lovely*

kaelan
still my favorite band

> *a moment*
> *and then*
> *the moment*
> *is broken*
> *as* **kaelan** *checks his watch*

luke
you look stressed

kaelan
yea
its like a fuckin war zone getting kids into a good school these days
they want to interview them
have them play with crayons and look at pictures
want to make sure their parents are well mannered
and well dressed and well heeled
and that the kids are taken care of and will grow up to be senators and
   cure diseases

you know because they can tell all of this from like age two
when theyre crawling around
in like diapers and stuff
its just

luke
you dont have to send him to a place like this

kaelan
public school
are you kidding me
yea right
then he'll end up at the bottom percentage
for like
for like
life you know
no
i cant have that
i have to give him all the things my parents didnt give me
things are going to be different with him
ill be different
thats important to me

luke
hey
you turned out pretty okay
and those cheekbones
they gave you a good jaw line

kaelan
thanks
i just want to be good for him you know

luke
you are

kaelan
you dont know that

luke
you wouldnt be here if you werent
                                    a moment

kaelan
its really good to see you

luke
thanks

you too
do you live nearby

kaelan
harlem

luke
uptown
fancy
nice

kaelan
where are you

luke
staten island

kaelan
oh
the island
i hear its a good investment
more room

luke
i like it
so

kaelan
so

luke
do you
do you maybe want to go out sometime

kaelan
like to lunch

luke
like on a date

kaelan
oh
i dont
i dont know

luke
yea totally
no big deal
i get it

kaelan
its not you
its just that
with my son
and work

luke
i understand

kaelan
it just seems like our lives are—

luke
right

kaelan
and when im not at the hospital working all those hours
i have to spend every minute of my time with him
you know
they dont stay young forever

luke
yea

kaelan
there never seems to be enough time
it just
it flies
man does it fly

luke
id really love to meet him

kaelan
definitely

luke
hey

kaelan
hey

luke
were adults

kaelan
doesnt feel like it

luke
tell me about it

a breath

luke
do you think its fate
us seeing each other here
like were tethered together or something

kaelan
you just said that
you really believe in stuff like that

luke
these days
i dont know what i believe anymore

a moment

kaelan
here they come
walking up
right there

luke
where

kaelan
thats my boy
thats my boy
thats my boy

and they wave

smiling

scene.

> the waiting room of a private clinic
> it is mostly calm and quiet
>> except for the sound of the television in the background
> maybe a baby crying
>> the sound of an elevator
>>> **vivienne** sits waiting
>>>> she stares out into nothingness
>> and then the sound of a phone ringing
>>> she pulls it out
>>>> about to answer
> looks at whos calling with a perplexed look on her face
>>>> and then silences it
> after a moment
>> the elevator opens and a handsome man in his thirties
> comes out
>> he seems rushed, disheveled

jack
vivienne
thank god youre here
i came as soon as i got your message

vivienne
i didnt mean to disrupt your day
its not a big deal

jack
of course it is

vivienne
im not scared

jack
i know youre not scared

vivienne
then

jack
youre so calm

vivienne
im sorry i alarmed you

jack
i just

vivienne
what

jack
i know youre not the most emotional person

vivienne
whats that supposed to mean

jack
you should be feeling things

vivienne
i am feeling things
dont tell me what im feeling
fuck do you think i am

jack
im your boyfriend

vivienne
not my father
see the distinction

jack
blow me

vivienne
watch it

jack
im sorry
im freaking out

vivienne
clearly

the phone rings
she looks at her phone again
confused look on her face

jack
what is it

vivienne
its my brother

jack
i thought you guys didnt really—

vivienne
me too

she silences the phone

jack
dont you think we should talk about this

vivienne
i wasnt feeling well
i got checked out
now im taking care of it

jack
i walk out of my meeting
look at my cellphone
missed call from my girlfriend
my girlfriend
who i happen to love very much
check your message
the words kept getting jumbled up in my head
they kept turning into static as you said them
i had to keep playing the message over and over and over
you know how many times i played it

vivienne
how many

jack
fourteen

vivienne
wow

jack
i had to play the message fourteen times just to understand what you
    were saying
now i may not be the most intellectually savvy person
but im not a total fuckin idiot
so
you can imagine
how hard it must have been to hear that

vivienne
oh was it
hard to hear that
because im the one who had to say it jack
me
im the one who said those words
not you
me
me
me

jack
ok
i get it

vivienne
do you
me
because i said it

jack
i got it

vivienne
good

jack
so what do we do

vivienne
we dont do anything

jack
so what do you do

vivienne
im doing it

jack
dont i have a say in this

vivienne
dont turn this into a fucking lifetime movie

jack
fuck off
im here
im not trying to make this harder

vivienne
then dont

jack
i just
i think we should talk about it

vivienne
we have
before

jack
that was then
this is now

vivienne
i dont want to have kids
it wasnt a secret the day you met me
it wasnt a secret on our first date or after our first kiss
it wasnt a secret the first time we slept together or when we decided to
    move in together
it was a conversation we had clearly
it was a conversation i was clear about
and one that you agreed on
i said i dont want to have kids
i cant
and you said okay
fine
i understand
i agree
i dont need them
thats fine
thats what you said
not once
or twice
but multiple times

jack
i thought

vivienne
what did you think

jack
people change
all the time

their thoughts
their opinions
they evolve
they digresss
i thought when this moment happened
any number of possibilities
could take shape
could manipulate the air around us
could turn you around

vivienne
this wasnt planned
or on purpose
it was something that happened
and now its going to be something thatll unhappen
and things can stay the same
its that simple

jack
its not that simple

vivienne
it is
IT IS

jack
you think im going to look at you the same

vivienne
what

jack
you think ill hear your voice the same way
that the image i have of you from last night and this morning and right
    now
will stay the same
it cant

vivienne
youre not the only one that can change things in his head jack

jack
just consider

vivienne
there is nothing to consider
you may be weak

jack
weak

vivienne
you may be weak but i am not
i know what i want
i cant
i wont

jack
please
just go home with me tonight

vivienne
i cant

jack
if you dont want to have it tomorrow
ill come back with you
ill be supportive
just go home
sleep on it

vivienne
no

jack
why not

vivienne
because i wouldnt be a good mother

jack
you dont know that

vivienne
because a child needs more emotion and attention than i am capable of
    giving

jack
false

vivienne
because we dont have enough space in our apartment

jack
well move

vivienne
because i cant stay at home and take care of the baby

jack
i will

vivienne
oh you will

jack
yes
besides these are all just stupid shitty excuses that any person can throw out
any person
who is
who is

vivienne
who is what

jack
acting like a coward

                              silence
                                        silence
                                                  silence

jack
i love you
but youre acting like a coward

                                        silence

vivienne
because we cant afford it

jack
ill get another job

vivienne
doing what
serving at a bar catering
as someones assistant
what are you qualified to do
maybe you can come into my office
and be my assistant
take down my coffee orders
thatll pay the bills

jack
ouch
ouch
fuck you
that was really

vivienne
its the truth

jack
i have a job

vivienne
designing sets
isnt exactly bringing in the health insurance and the big paycheck now
    is it

jack
i didnt know you had a problem with my job

vivienne
i dont

jack
it sure sounds like you do

vivienne
if it makes you happy
its what makes me happy
so im happy for you

jack
bullshit

vivienne
i love your job
i love that youre an artist and do what you want
i love that
but its not enough
for this
for a baby
for a family
its not enough

jack
youre miserable arent you

vivienne
excuse me

jack
i did what i wanted with my life
and you resent me for that
that unlike you
i didnt take some shitty job

vivienne
that shitty job pays for everything you have

jack
im sorry that you wanted to be a photographer and you didnt do it
im sorry that you didnt have the balls to do what you want in this life

vivienne
fuck you
you dont know a thing
you dont know what it means to be an adult
to make sacrifices
youre just some silly overgrown child
trying to play adult
you know nothing

silence

silence

jack
if im not good enough
why are you with me

vivienne
i wish i could do this without hurting you
but i cant

jack
you could have picked anybody else

vivienne
i picked you

jack
and what if i want to have a baby

vivienne
then youre with the wrong person

jack
how do you know that

vivienne
because ive already made up my mind

jack
i dont believe you

vivienne
when someone tells you who they are
or what they want
you should believe them

jack
i love you

> *she looks at him*
> > *she looks at him*
> *and starts to cry*
> > *she doesnt wail or scream or moan or have*
> *a breakdown*
> > *its very soft*
> *its very held back*
> > *a moment*
> > > *and then*
> > > *the sound of a text on a phone*
> **vivienne** *looks at it*

vivienne
WHAT DO YOU WANT
> *and then everything SHATTERS*

jack
what is it
what does it say

vivienne
its my mother
i have to go

jack
wait

vivienne
i cant do this right now

jack
when someone tells you—

> *and then*
>> *that terrible overwhelming static noise*
>
> *as* **jack** *becomes*
>> **old-fashioned traveling salesman**

jack/traveling salesman
you should believe them

> *blackout*

scene.

> **vivienne** *wears all black*
> *there is a giant beautiful tree near her*
> *she is wearing shades and her arms are crossed*
> *after a moment*
> **derek** *enters*

derek
you look beautiful

vivienne
what are you doing here

derek
came to pay my respects

vivienne
thank you

derek
im sorry for your loss

vivienne
really

derek
thats what youre supposed to say isnt it
thats the tradition

vivienne
traditions are stupid

derek
not all of them

vivienne
you always were old fashioned
always did what mom and dad wanted you to do

derek
theyve set me off on the right path

vivienne
hows california

derek
ive been back for a while now
in the old neighborhood

a block from my parents
they need me you know
its important to be close to family

vivienne
look at you

derek
im an engineer now

vivienne
of course you are

derek
what about you

vivienne
i moved to chicago

derek
chicago
really

vivienne
i wanted to get lost somewhere
reinvent myself

derek
and did you

vivienne
no

derek
what do you do

vivienne
youll never guess

derek
youre a lawyer

vivienne
me
a lawyer

derek
you were always strong
had some fight in you

vivienne
im a photographer

derek
well look at you
a grown-up photographer

vivienne
i didnt say grown-up
its a good hobby though

derek
so then what

vivienne
im a professor of mathematics

derek
and are you happy viv

a moment

vivienne
are you

a moment
and then
they hug awkwardly

derek
well its good to see you

vivienne
you too derek

and then he goes
she stands there in silence for a moment
and then
luke *arrives*

luke
staying long

vivienne
no
im going back tomorrow

luke
quick trip

vivienne
only came to bury mother
say goodbye one last time

luke
i cant believe she killed herself

vivienne
dramatic till the end

luke
she would do that
she would kill herself

vivienne
she did

a moment

vivienne
what arent you telling me

luke
nothing

a moment

luke
she was sick

vivienne
sick
sick how

luke
she had cancer

vivienne
what kind

luke
does it matter
the bad kind

vivienne
i didnt know

luke
of course you didnt

vivienne
whats that supposed to mean

luke
she didnt want you to know vivienne
i dont even know why she told me

vivienne
so she killed herself
didnt want anyone to see her deteriorate from the beautiful
perfect thing that she was
makes sense

luke
youre wrong you know

vivienne
then why

luke
because we abandoned her viv
because she had no one left
because unlike the other chinese families that she knew
her kids werent around to make sure she didnt die alone
the shame in that

vivienne
in the end its always about shame
well i didnt know

luke
would it have changed anything
                              silence

luke
she died alone viv
alone
the worst kind of death
dont worry
i wasnt here either

vivienne
so thats it huh
a whole life lived

                         silence
            silence
                    silence

vivienne
i miss dad

                                        a moment

luke
kaelan came
he has this whole other life
what if
what if
this is all there is
its just who we are
what if its just in our character
what if this is who you are
and who i am
and who he is
what if theres no changing things
what if its too late
and ive already missed out on
what if no one ever looks at me
what if thats not even the point
to be something to someone
to be anything
what if the things we want will never fit together

vivienne
youre asking the wrong person

                silence as they look at the old neighborhood
                                the sounds in the distance
                        of laughing children
                                of the wind blowing
                                        of family
                                                of life
                        the old one
                                the one that never changes

luke
so

vivienne
so

luke
whats new
anything new with you

vivienne
yea
yea there is

luke
what

> *they stand in silence*
> *we hear the birds*
> *and the trees rustling*
> *and the wind*
> *the wind picks up*
> *and it blows some leaves*
> *. . . the leaves and the wind*
> *and the wind*
> *and the wind*
> *until the leaves are everywhere*
> *so many leaves*
> *so many leaves everywhere*
> *and the wind*
> *so much wind*
> *until they are just covered . . .*
> *and disappear*
> *blackout*

END OF ACT THREE

epilogue.

scene.

> *the future*
> **luke** *wears a suit and tie*
> *he sits in a beautiful office with floor-to-ceiling windows*
> *the views outside the window are stunning*
> *they are really high up*
> *its not new york*
> *its not even america*
> *were in china now*
> **sonya washington** *sits in front of* **luke**
> *she is a powerful woman*
> *in a powerful suit*
> *in a powerful position*
> *in a powerful company*

sonya
youre fluent in four languages

luke
english
spanish
i can speak cantonese AND mandarin
and i also know some french and german

sonya
impressive

luke
i also know some asl

sonya
your degrees and your grades speak for themselves

luke
thank you

sonya
and you really want to be here
in china

luke
its a beautiful place

and my family
this is where they came from
so im home in a sense
and this company

sonya
this company

luke
is at the forefront of the global market
what you do here

sonya
is ahead of the game

luke
its remarkable
theres nowhere else id rather be
a hundred percent
i am committed to being a part of this company and being the best
    employee possible
i will work tirelessly for you
my skills—

sonya
speak for themselves

luke
i think youll find that ill be an excellent addition to this corporation

sonya
to this monolith
                        there is a knock at the door

sonya
one moment please

luke
absolutely

sonya
come in

                    william grant *enters the office*
                        he is very familiar
                            a tinge of purple

william
i have that information you asked about

sonya
and

william
well

> *he puts a file on her desk*
> *and then whispers in her ear*
> *a sharp static fills the air*
> *as he whispers he points at different things in the files*
> *different pages*
> *her face becomes dismayed*

sonya
mister andrews

luke
anthony
please call me anthony

sonya
mister anthony andrews
this is my collague

luke
its nice to meet you

> *a look*

luke
you look familiar
have we met before

> *a look*

luke
at one of my previous interviews here maybe

william
highly unlikely
i just started working here
i used to work in insurance
back when it meant something

sonya
not anymore

william
not anymore

luke
i dont think i caught your name

sonya
hes one of our in-house research specialists

luke
oh
interesting
what kind of research do you do

william
people research
you for instance

luke
me
sure
like where i went to school
and my grades and such

william
its a little bit more personal im afraid

sonya
my colleague has brought me some interesting
finds
well call them finds about you
finds that
honestly

luke
finds
what finds

sonya
well for one
mister anthony andrews
it says here your given name is luke wood

luke
it was
my name was luke wood
but i changed it a long time ago
everything in those files
my grades
languages

accomplishments
theye all mine
i just
i changed my name

sonya
why

luke
it didnt fit

william
it didnt fit

sonya
thats interesting isnt it

william
it is
it didnt fit or you wanted to be someone else

luke
i wanted to start over
be better
be different

sonya
unfortunately
mister wood
mister luke wood
thats not possible
you cant just become someone else whenever you want
and so now that this new setback has presented itself

william
we have to review your file
together

sonya
my colleague has been a busy man
havent you

william
i certainly have

sonya
and youve found some interesting things like this
looks like some kind of party

and there is
well

william
theres a lot of cocaine in that picture with you mister wood

luke
let me see that

she hands it to him

luke
that was a long time ago
at a college party
and it wasnt even mine
i didnt even know that picture existed

william
thats what im here for

sonya
he can find anything on the internet
anything on the server
anything on the ether about you

luke
this picture

sonya
could make the company look bad
irresponsible
if those are the types of people we are hiring
drug addicts

luke
im not a drug addict

sonya
what you do behind closed doors is your business

william
just dont get caught

luke
one picture

sonya
oh theres more

luke
more

william
this business with your sister
a
what did you call it
a dick-sucking list

sonya
that is really inappropriate mister wood
makes me feel really uncomfortable when i have to hear those words

luke
i was a kid

sonya
kid or no kid mister wood

william
what you do is going to follow you forever

luke
i didnt know

sonya
the fact that you would do this
to your own family
it seems like you dont have any
whats the word im looking for

william
loyalty

sonya
exactly
how can we hire someone we cant even trust
so many precious secrets
so much information
at this corporation

william
this monolith

sonya
whoever works with us must be trusted

william
can you be trusted mister wood

luke
i can

i can

william
well see about that

sonya
we have a lot of files to go through

william
youve been a very very busy man mister wood

sonya
shut the door will you
this might take a while

> **the tiger** *appears*
> *unseen to the characters*
> *maybe as before*
> *maybe broken and disheveled*
> *now less powerful . . .*
> *powerless?*

the tiger
as the door slowly shuts
    we watch for a brief moment as they begin to go over the files
luke sits in his chair
                        uncomfortable
                                sad
                    terrified
                            broken

luke
i just want it to go away
i just want it to go away

the tiger
            but it doesnt
                    it never does
            not anymore
                            blackout

END OF PLAY